ORVIS®

The Orvis Guide to
Personal
Fishing Craft

How to Effectively Fish from Canoes, Kayaks, and Inflatables

RICKEY NOEL MITCHELL

The Lyons Press
Guilford, Connecticut
An imprint of The Globe Pequot Press

To buy books in quantity for corporate use
or incentives, call **(800) 962–0973**
or e-mail **premiums@GlobePequot.com**.

The Lyons Press is an imprint of The Globe Pequot Press.

10 9 8 7 6 5 4 3 2 1

Printed in the United States of America

Library of Congress Cataloging-in-Publication Data

Mitchell, Rickey Noel.
   The Orvis guide to personal fishing craft : how to effectively fish from
canoes, kayaks, and inflatables / Rickey Noel Mitchell.
      p. cm.
   Includes index.
   ISBN 978-1-59228-813-7
   1. Fishing boats. I. Orvis Company. II. Title.
   SH452.9.B58M58 2007
   799.1028'4—dc22

                        2007026921

Dedicated to one who teaches
And one who creates.
Both are my life's inspiration.
(My wife Elaina Marlene Smith,
and daughter, Megan Beth Mitchell)
From he who now writes.

Contents

Acknowledgments

Special thanks to Amy Marie Jenkins, who could easily be the world's best assistant, for modeling and learning to paddle any craft I asked her to, as well as for assisting in the setup of crafts for this book and for her genuine desire and passion to learn the art of fly fishing and paddling. Thank you to William Jenkins (1949–2007) for teaching Amy to cast a fly.

Thanks to my best friend Kevin Human for being there when I needed him.

I am also indebted to Ken Hanley for years of his invaluable counsel as well as his encouragement with this book. He inspired me to pursue writing about fly fishing, and has always been generous with his knowledge and expertise.

My deepest appreciation is extended to:

Weldon Schapansky for the privilege of photographing, fishing and paddling his beautiful waters, and to his son Scott for being one of my best fly-tying students and for the honor of being his teacher and friend.

Many thanks to the kayak makers for the use of their kayaks: Cathy Weil and John from Wilderness Systems, Mark Olson and Jeff Kriger (also known as "the Rhyno") from Ocean Kayak, and Sean Caples from Malibu kayaks.

Ted Thibault of Bottom Line fishfinders (makers of the Fishin' Buddy), Bob Sharten and Bob Ross from Herb Bauer's Sporting Goods for loaning me float tubes and kayaks, Eric Kaai from Fishermen's Warehouse, and Kurt Renner and Bill Kueper from Current Designs Kayaks and Wenonah Canoes.

I've had no formal training with the Greenland Paddle. The knowledge I share with you in Chapter 5 comes from time, trial and error on the water,

Acknowledgments

and a generous sharing of knowledge from a wonderful website called Qaan-nat Kattuffiat (www.qajaqusa.org). Qaannat Kattuffiat, the Greenland Kayaking Association, is a Greenland-based organization that is dedicated to keeping the traditional kayaking skills of Greenland alive.

Last but not least, my deepest gratitude to Gary and Lisa Sinkus for inspiring me back in the 1980s to cast a line from a kayak, and Tom Rosenbauer for the opportunity and privilege of writing this book.

Introduction

In my search for the perfect platform from which to cast a fishing line, I've paddled a plethora of floating objects on California waters. It all began with a float tube, which, while not the most versatile craft in all waters, is a most convenient craft. I could throw my tube and gear in a trunk or truck bed, and be off. Sitting on the water (in the case of the float tube, in the water), and fighting fish from the tube is simply fantastic. It doesn't take a big fish to pull you around in the float tube, and it can get you places where a boat can't go.

For me, the float tube's biggest plus is to be able to position yourself in the water using your feet. While my fishing improved, however, my casting did not. Making a cast while sitting low in the water isn't easy, to say nothing of the effort involved in paddling from point A to point Z.

Another choice I had in the selection of inflatable crafts was the pontoon boat, which is two cylindrical objects held together by an aluminum frame and a couple of inflatable bladders. Whether I set up my pontoon at home, or on the shore of the water I was going to fish, it took at least an hour to set it up. I love to sight fish, to move across the water silently until I catch sight of a good fish, and then stalk close enough for a cast. But when you row or paddle a pontoon over the water, the movement causes a noisy slap. When it came to stalking big fish from a pontoon, the sight of them was all I could catch, and that was usually of their tails disappearing into deeper water. As time went by I began to understand the pros and cons of fishing from a pontoon. As a river craft, a pontoon boat can be pure heaven. On open water such as large reservoirs—especially with a good strong wind—they can be pure hell.

The pontoon would not be the last craft I paddled before encountering the kayak. The final vessel I paddled before the kayak (and one that I've used throughout my life and consider second only to the 'yak) is the canoe. With a history as rich and almost as old as kayaking and predating fly fishing substantially, the canoe has been with fly fishing throughout the latter's history and is still an integral part of it. With a good paddler in the stern seat, the canoe can be the perfect fly-fishing vessel for the angler casting from the bow. And a lone angler in a canoe can have a good day of fishing all by him- or herself, as long the wind doesn't blow too hard or he has a good anchor system.

But my search for the perfect fishing platform ended with my own discovery of a craft created a few thousand years ago: the kayak. I wanted a craft from which I could cast my line in all waters—reservoirs, rivers, and even the ocean. After several years and several crafts, the kayak is that craft.

All fish cannot be reached from shore.
For a fisherman to be complete
He must go upon the water.
Rickey Noel Mitchell

The Float Tube

The float tube is a craft that enables you to position yourself in the water using only your feet, while your hands are free to cast. It's like casting from your favorite easy chair.

Getting into the water, however, can be a whole different matter. If your tube is the traditional style, start close to the water's edge. Put your fins on, carefully step into the doughnut, slide it up around your belly, and carefully walk backwards into the water. While you're walking backwards with fins on, be careful with your rod. Always carry your rod handle in hand, tip pointed

The doughnut.

forward, as you walk backwards. This simple technique could save your rod should you fall.

Do not—I repeat, do NOT—try to walk forward in a pair of fins; you'll be asking for disaster.

With the more modern styles of float tube, the problems of walking backwards or breaking your rod can be avoided. All you do is simply sit down in your seat, put your fins on, and push yourself into deeper water. But whatever style of tube you choose, once in the water it will be like floating in air. The fins on your feet will be your power as you glide slowly through the water, casting toward shore or working the edge of a weed bed. (On the subject of casting in a float tube, a few quick thrusts with your fin-adorned feet and you can always make room for a good back cast. See Chapter 2 for more on fishing techniques in this type of watercraft.) Prices of float tubes range from under a hundred dollars for the traditional donut style to over three hundred for some of the more modern varieties. Not a bad price for a craft that can go places where a boat can't go, and which you can carry over your shoulder.

Over the years, the belly boat has evolved from its perfectly round O-shape into newer U, V, and even H shapes. New designs and trends have caused the classic belly boat to fall by the wayside, but not for everybody. Lee Haskins, one of California's most noted and veteran float-tube anglers, is very familiar with the well-known waters of San Luis Reservoir and O'Neill Forebay, where several IGFA fly-fishing records have been caught from a float tube. Since these areas can be very windy, fishing with the wind is a constant issue, and Haskins has found that the round donut-style float tube is the lowest-profile tube available. Pontoons or U-boats, which have sides with more surface area to catch a breeze, can be tough to control when the wind hits the craft. Typically, these vessels sit higher in the water, presenting a bigger target—as well as more of the fisherman—to the wind.

"In a round float tube, I can brace my knees against the bottom of the tube for leverage when kicking down," says Haskins. He also finds that this helps conserve energy, and gives him more power in each kick. With this technique he can hold his position in waves, continuing to fish, while other crafts would require more energy to maintain position.

"If you were in a U-boat you would have to paddle from your hip, which provides less power, and is more exhausting. In choppy waters you can take a hit from a wave from any direction and still hold your position."

Another advantage of float tubes over other crafts is increased launching options. There are few other craft that you can carry like a backpack, and walk past the long line at the boat launches to the water or hike in to your favorite spot. Wind and waves rarely stop Haskins from fishing. He'll judge the direction of the wind and select a launch point, which gives him an easy entry and allows him to kick across the waves, to the target fishing area. Once in position, he can then hold his position against the wind and waves, and use the former to assist his casting. The wind direction and strength always dictate the areas he fishes on both impoundments.

Round floats use a truck tube, which is easy to repair and replace. Bladders, especially custom products, are quite expensive, and the seams have been known to fail and cause a quick deflation. Truck tubes do not have seams, and leaks are usually very small and insignificant. Haskins, in addition to the truck tube, uses an old truck tube, cut in half, as a sheath in the front half of the tube to protect it from fish-mediated punctures. This is a constant problem with striped bass, a primary target species in his home waters.

There are advantages to the U- or H-shaped float tube. You can put one in the water, sit down in it, and then put your fins on. Some of the first U-boats (as they were called when they first came out) had a flaw. When an angler sat down in his tube, the two ends would collapse inward. The problem was corrected by installing a bar

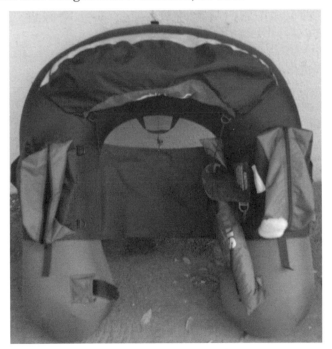

U-boat.

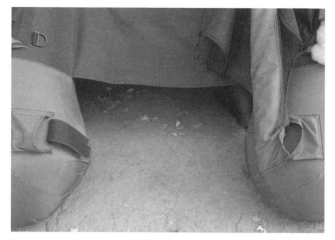

The bar

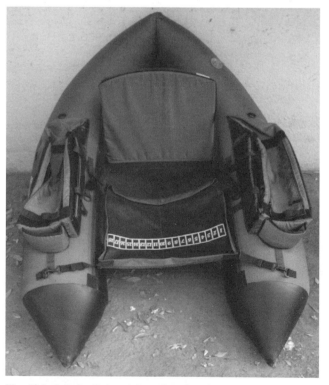

The Fish Cat, by Outcast Sporting Goods.

that was permanently fastened to one end. The other end could be connected to the other side, once the angler was seated. If that particular U-boat design is your choice, make sure it has the bar. But the ability to sit down in your tube and then put your fins on isn't the only advantage of the U-boat.

The design of the Fish Cat float tube by Outcast Sporting Goods, actually shaped more like an A than a U, enables you to sit higher in the water. The back ends of the Fish Cat are welded together, providing a storage area in back and a higher, firmer casting chair. I have found that the A-shape helps you to move through the water a bit faster than the O- or the older U-shaped tubes.

While it may lack an aluminum frame, the Orvis Day Tripper float is more pontoon boat than float tube. The Day Tripper's H-shape is formed by a foam seat with a pontoon sewn on each side of it. Another U-shaped tube, with storage bags incorporated into its design, is strapped down on top of it with hook-and-loop straps. On land, the Day Tripper resembles an easy chair more than any other tube design I've seen. In the water, it sits low enough such that you have excellent control with your fins, yet high enough to ensure that your casting isn't hampered.

A word of warning is advised. When driving up to those mountain lakes or streams, deflate your tubes or pontoon bladders to about three-quarters of their normal size. Because they expand at higher elevations, there is a definite risk of over-inflation, and possibly bursting, that could occur.

The bladders of entry-level float tubes and pontoons are usually made of vinyl. Such a bladder will do the job of holding air, but it will not have the durability of urethane. Highly resistant to any puncture or

The Orvis Day Tripper float tube.

moisture, urethane is considered the state-of-the-art material in bladder construction. Higher-priced U-boats' and pontoons' bladders are usually made of urethane (also known as polyurethane).

For all your locomotion—getting from shore to your fishing spot, getting back again, or holding your position once you get there—you will be wearing your paddling power on your feet. For me, one of the biggest pluses in a float tube or a pontoon boat is having my hands free for casting, while my feet are doing the work. And it is the fins that make this possible.

There are two makes of fins with which I'm familiar: Caddis Float Tube Fins, which are around $30, and Force Fins for $100 and up. Caddis Fins are basic conventional fins that will do the job, although they are somewhat stiff compared to the flexible and light Force Fins. Stiff fins make for stiff paddling, while flexible ones bend as you draw your foot back for your paddle stroke and stiffen out when you push forward, providing you with more efficient paddling.

Float tube fins. The pair on the left are by Caddis; the pair on the right are Force Fins.

The beauty of float tubes is their simplicity; they don't take a lot of skill. Once in the water, just paddle backwards; to turn around simply paddle with one foot. Within an hour it will be second nature. Before you know it, your natural abilities and your flipper-adorned feet will have you moving through the water like a duck.

I do recommend that you take the care of your float tube seriously, because they can leak. Never go so far from shore that you couldn't make it back if your tube did rupture.

Float tubes can be used in a wide variety of waters, starting with ponds. Ponds and float tubes were meant for each other; a body of water too small for a boat, too deep to wade, and full of fish was probably the inspiration for the first float tube's creation. Lakes are well within the purview of the float tuber also. As long as you use caution when you paddle a float tube, you can safely take advantage of all the possibilities and adventure a large freshwater lake or reservoir has to offer.

Rivers require more caution, and you should know the stretch of river you're targeting. Rivers collect objects such as fallen trees and who-knows-what-else after flood season. Submerged trees or stumps and strong current have claimed the lives of numerous unfortunate anglers. Consider the following story, which I heard years ago. A man was floating down a river, and got caught in a strong current that dragged him into a submerged tree. The current was enough to flip him upside down, and a limb from the tree caught and held him in that position long enough to drown him.

The float tube (left) and pontoon boat (right), when fully rigged.

How about the ocean? People do float tube in salt water, but the hazards are real. It's not too unusual to read about the fly slinger who hooks a big fish, and gets towed so far out to sea that he almost loses sight of land. You won't catch me doing a seal imitation in California shore waters. The ocean surf can, and has, tossed float tubers around like beach balls. Those currents and tides can be far more dangerous then anything that swims within.

Wind is rarely a problem for the float tube–situated angler. When a strong wind blows, put your back to it, holding position with your feet while your hands are free to cast. You will be able to stay squarely on that hot spot, better than any fisherman casting a line from a boat.

RIGGING YOUR FLOAT TUBE AND PONTOON BOAT

The simplest of personal crafts should be rigged, well, simply, and this is the beauty of the float tube. A good quality float tube is going to have pockets for storing fly boxes, lunch, and other gear. So the list of after-market accessories needed for rigging your craft should be small: two rod holders at the most, net, fish finder, and anchor. Remember: you want to be able to put it in your car or truck, head for your favorite waters, and be fishing a half hour or less after you get there.

A Personal Flotation Device (PFD) is worth careful consideration. If your inflatable craft springs a leak while in the middle of a lake, you're going to have to swim, and there's all your gear—not to mention your safety—to worry about. Can you think of a better time to have a life jacket on?

Fish finders can be a great help. Bottom Line's Fishin' Buddy with its tube adapter has always been popular with tubers. In the past few years, however, I'm seeing a lot more fishermen using console models on float tubes and pontoon boats, with adapters either acquired commercially or home-made.

These options will serve in a pontoon boat as well, but in these craft it's easier to remember to lift your Fishin' Buddy out of its holder and not risk damage to the shaft, if you accidentally drag it over the bottom. In a pontoon boat you're going to be moving faster when traveling from the launch point to your fishing spot and back again. Remember to remove the Fishin' Buddy from its holder.

Net or BogaGrip: I use both on a pontoon boat. After losing several fish right by my craft (or having them wind up in my lap) because I couldn't get to my net in time or the rod leash got tangled, I started using a Scotty's conventional rod holder for my net, and now my sanity is safe. In a float tube you might want to use a shorter-handled net. While I have a high opinion of the BogaGrip, I like a longer reach in a tube or a pontoon boat, because I've had more than one good-size fish hogtie me with my fly line. If you use a BogaGrip in a tube, remember a leash or lanyard. (The BogaFloat, an accessory product, can also be used to keep the BogaGrip from disappearing into the depths.)

The largemouth bass is but one of the many fish species that can be targeted when fishing from a pontoon boat.

Storage: As far as storage goes, most pontoons have a storage bag you hook-and-loop fasten, or buckle down, for each pontoon.

Accessory choices you made for your float tube will serve you just as well on your pontoon boat. So I will not repeat myself in the list below.

Rod Holders: For about twenty-five bucks, Scotty's fly rod holder with its float tube adapter can't be beat.

Leashes: Many a float tuber's rod has found its way to the bottom of a river or a lake when he was changing a fly or taking a picture. A leash avoids this.

Fly Boxes or tackle bags: The float tube can function as a floating tackle bag that carries your gear as well as you. All I ever take is the box of flies I'll need. Bags that can be fastened to the pontoons are usually included with the pontoon boat.

The Pontoon Boat 2

Another versatile choice in inflatable crafts is the pontoon boat, two cylinder-shaped inflatable objects in various lengths, held together by an aluminum frame, with a nice comfortable chair. You can sit down in that chair and put your fins on, rather than walking backwards into the water. Further, your position is high enough so that you're completely out of the water, yet low enough so you can still use fin power to position your pontoon boat. Alternately, you can rest your feet on the footrest and use oars for power.

For an angler wanting a more convenient but still versatile craft, a pontoon boat could be the best choice. Available from six to twelve feet in length, a deflated and unassembled pontoon boat can fit in a car trunk. They can be outfitted with an electric motor, fish finder, and oars, and they're one of the most stable crafts afloat.

The overall design of pontoon boats varies little. When you are ready to purchase your first one, the length should be the determining factor. For example, a seven-foot pontoon boat will turn much more easily than a ten-foot one. On the other hand, the ten-footer will track better than a shorter one, but it will not be as easy to hold a steady position in the water with your fins because of its size. My choice of length for these H-shaped crafts is a seven-footer. I can hold my position in the water or float down my favorite river, and it's easy to carry or load it on top of my truck.

Most pontoon boats can be inflated, set up, and made ready to go in about thirty minutes. A real time saver, if you do not have the convenience of a pickup bed or trailer, is a car roof rack. You can set the pontoon up at home the night before, thus maximizing you fishing time when you reach your destination.

Ponds and lakes can both be fished via these craft, but the one can be too small and the other too large. On a small pond, pontoons can be overkill—if you have a float tube in your fleet of crafts, use it instead.

As for lakes, I recall one particular day. It was not a bad day for fishing; I rolled into a cove and into a school of shad-busting bass. I caught three largemouths, one right after another, and then a bigger bass took my fly and promptly broke me off. I had been holding my position with my feet, and in my excitement and haste to tie another fly on, I took my feet out of the water. Once I had my fly tied on, I looked up. The cove I had been fishing was growing smaller in the distance as I was being blown toward the middle of the lake.

Stick with early morning, smooth water, or paddling along the shore, working coves or docks. Stay away from wind and large bodies of water. Open waters and high winds can conspire to reduce your pontoon boat to a wind toy.

Rivers are where the creation of the pontoon craft was inspired.

Loaded down and ready to go.

When you sit on a couple of inflated bladders as you float down a fast river, stability isn't an issue. However, good paddling skills are, and with them you can float down rivers with rapids from Class I to IV. Unless an obstacle in your path is above the water line, the pontoon boat will flow right over it.

Ocean angling with a pontoon might be possible, but all due caution must be observed. It's probably best to restrict yourself to bays; a lot of pontoon boat anglers and float tubers do fish bays, usually locals that know their waters and have good paddling skills. Be safe.

Wind is something that must be taken into account. My first time on a large body of water in a pontoon was when I came up with the term "wind toy." As mentioned previously, in a pontoon you're completely out of the water, as are the pontoons themselves (except for a few inches.) Any time you stop paddling or rowing, if the wind is blowing, you will be blown across the water like you have a sail unless you have a good anchor set up.

As I mentioned before, the length of pontoon boats vary from six feet to twelve. For the best

Use your thumbs to help with proper oar adjustment.

Collar rings for your oars help to keep them secure.

maneuverability in these vessels, eight feet is a good all-around length as it will track and turn well.

The oars for this size craft need be no longer than six feet. To adjust the oars for your arm length, position yourself in place, holding the oars. During the power stroke, extend your two thumbs toward each other, and when they are closest to each other they should just touch.

Additionally, your oars should have collars on them. An oar collar or ring is a rubber ring that you can slip down around the oar shaft to stop it from slipping into the water through the oarlocks. You can tighten the collar so that it stays in place, using the nuts and bolts incorporated in the design. Once the collars are locked down in the chosen position on the oar handles, you won't have to worry about losing the oars. . . or banging your hands together when you're rowing, for that matter. When you're ready to cast a line, all you have to do is lift your oars up out of the water and rest them on the frame, or leave them in the water to slow your craft's drift.

Rowing a pontoon boat is straightforward and easy to learn. Once on the water—leaning forward with oar handles in hands, oar blades pointed behind you and out of the water, your feet braced firmly against the footrests—lower the oar blades into the water. You'll now pull backwards and somewhat upwards, and you will be propelling your craft

Line your knuckles up with the edge of the blade.

across the water backwards, which is the most effective way in a pontoon boat. To row forward, sit back in your chair with your oar handles in hands, blades pointed forward out of the water with your feet braced firmly against the footrests, lower the oar blades into the water, push forward, and you'll propel yourself forward. The first thing you'll discover is you won't have the same power that you had when you pulled to move backwards.

The pontoon boat is clearly not a craft for all water; however, rivers and pontoons were tailor-made for each other. Going down a river, carried by a good current, using the occasional brace stroke with the oar to keep your craft on course as you work the edges, can be pure Heaven. A more advanced technique is a rowing method that works well going forward or in reverse. I call it the "rolling row" for lack of a better

Pontoon boat rowing efficiency is maximized if the rower's knuckles are aligned with the blade.

name. It is easiest learned by watching a demonstration, but in brief it can be described as follows: Start with oars in hand, extended out to each side of you, knuckles lined up with the edge of the blades. With the oars in the water, push forward with one hand and then the other, or pull backward, depending on which direction you wish to go. Rowing hand over hand, you'll glide over the water. Form the habit of burying your blade in the water and then lifting at the end of the stroke, and you will be able to use stealth when fishing from a pontoon boat. The stroke you'll need for those times that you

Rolling row stroke

need to turn, such as dodging boulders or other obstacles in the middle of a river—or simply turning around—is called the brace stroke. When you're rowing along at a pretty good pace and you need to turn, firmly hold one paddle in the water (bracing), and lift the other out of the water. If you want to turn right brace right; if you want to turn left brace left.

Fishing Techniques for the Float Tube and Pontoon Boat

Because of the simplicity of the float tube and the stability of the pontoon boat, you will be able to apply the casting abilities you've attained throughout your fly-fishing career when you sit down in either of these crafts. Please remember: in any of these crafts, for the sake of safety and your sanity, watch your back cast.

How many times have you hooked a fish when you were dragging your fly in the water, either from a boat or while wading? Now imagine doing it on purpose with planned techniques. In the tube (or kick boat, as it is sometimes affectionately called) you will feel that beloved strike when the fish hits because your hands will be free. You will be able to hold your rod in your hands while you give your fly life with those flipper-adorned feet. The situation can be the same in your pontoon boat if you are controlling it similarly.

Anchoring is something that merits preparation. My personal choice for a float tube is no anchor at all; your fins will do a good enough job of keeping you where the fish are. Anchors for float tubes, however, are available, and any good-quality pontoon frame will have a set up for anchor system.

If you opt to use an anchor system on a float tube, don't just keep it simple; keep it small. You will be carrying it on your tube. A three-pound anchor

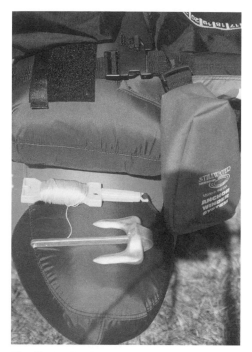

The float tube anchor.

Pontoon boat anchor.

and twenty feet of rope is more than adequate. I prefer to omit the anchor on a float tube because, as the smallest personal fishing craft, you and the anchor rope will never be more than two feet from each other. This presents a situation that can work in favor of the fish. Consider the case in which I had a brown trout tie the anchor rope and my leg together with my line, as well as the fact that I've had to strip in more than one fish with the anchor rope because they wrapped the fly line around it.

Since you can hold your position in the water with a pair of flippers on your feet, in both the float tube and the pontoon boat, why would you need an anchor system on either of them? I'll answer this question with another question. What fish-eating predator do you think you sound like as you propel yourself through, or position yourself in, the water with your flippers?

Cormorants. These are birds that can swim under the water as well as they can fly. After landing on the water, a cormorant will skid across the surface, and then come to rest on the water. It will paddle around and then dive, repeating this procedure until success is achieved. Rarely have I seen a cormorant surface without a fish in its bill, thanks in large part to its big, webbed feet.

On one occasion in the early morning, I was just about ready to cast to some largemouth bass that had been busting bait, when a cormorant landed some distance away and started swimming in the direction of the bass. Hidden behind a tree, I had a clear view of it all. The bass spooked when they detected the bird's presence. As the cormorant swam toward the bass, its paddling reminded me somewhat of myself when I'm in a float tube. . . although, of course, I'm nowhere near as graceful. The cormorant dove beneath the surface, and then surfaced a few moments later with what looked like a two-pound bass in its bill.

The shadow a predator casts scares fish as much as their swimming motions. Human shadows cast a much bigger shadow in a float tube or kick boat, and presumably scare fish that much more. The cormorant is probably the best example of what we sound like as we move through the water with our fin-clad feet.

What does any of this have to do with anchors? In any personal paddle craft a good anchor system will hold your position, allowing the angler to use substantially less motion. Paddle or row as silently as possible within casting distance of your favorite structure, and carefully drop anchor. In a float tube, just let your legs hang still. If you're sitting in a pontoon boat put your feet on the footrest. Once you are anchored and in position, do not move those fins; if you're not moving them you will not be making the sounds of a predator. Floating motionlessly, you'll resemble a floating log or even a small weed bed. After a while, the fish will go about their business, thinking you're simply some structure. Do not move your legs, the only movement should be casting your line.

FISHING TACTICS

Working with Current and Covering Water

Current can provide float tube and pontoon boat anglers with challenges and advantages. Their main performance aspect—paddling backwards—is the essential key to fishing. As stated earlier, holding a position in the current in a float tube can be achieved by using your fins to propel and stabilize yourself, and also create drag and act as rudders. In a pontoon boat, just backpaddle, or use one paddle to swing against the current, using the drag to turn your position if you're trying to get a better shot at a cast, or are fighting a fish.

Example: You're paddling a pontoon boat and casting in a workable current; "workable" meaning that you can paddle against the current (if you can't, you shouldn't be there in the first place). As the current carries you along, you get a good hit but miss the fish. Back paddle to a point above the strike zone, then ride the current down again, casting with one arm while using the other to paddle with a slight churning stroke to regulate your speed relative to the drift of your fly, if the current in the strike zone is slower than where you are. In a float tube, come into the strike zone facing at a slight downstream angle (about 40 degrees) and paddle with your fins to control your speed. As you reach the tail of the run, use your fins to turn your body at an angle upstream to get one last shot.

When you ride currents faster than the current where the fish are (behind rocks, in eddies, or along undercut banks) you're going to have to be a quick caster—pick your targets, ride through, and take your shots. A combination of mending and a little paddle work can let you drift a fly through a long section without getting drag.

Example: As you ride down the middle of a river, you see to your left a stretch of shoreline that looks promising (call it point A to point Z). Paddle toward the opposite shoreline, and then turn and paddle upriver, getting above point A. Drift down to within casting distance of point A, and pick your targets—up to two or three, like plotting your shots in a game of 8-Ball—and make your casts. Or, if your speed matches the speed of the fly, drift that whole section, letting the current take you all the way to point Z.

Fighting and Landing Big Fish

Hooking and fighting a big fish in current, with both the fish and you moving along, is a somewhat odd experience the first time it happens, as most of us are used to fighting a fish from a fixed position on two feet. In a sense, you've got to counter-swim with and against the fish.

When the fight is on, first paddle backwards, away from the spot of the strike, pulling the fish away from any structure he could use to break you off. If the fish is of some size, he might start surging downstream. Let him take you along; don't paddle against him to try to wear him out—he'll do that himself. If a big fish dives and bulldogs you, and you're in a belly boat, you can use your fins to help keep the line taut if the fish swims toward you or below you by paddling away from him. In a pontoon boat, fight him as you would if you were wading, keeping the line taut, but also, more importantly, keep the rod bent—don't point the rod at the fish as you reel. And in either case, if the fish wants to go into cover, lower the rod to the side, keeping it bent, and turn the fish away from snags.

One note: On rivers or streams with quick currents, keep an eye on your downstream path as the fish runs and fights. More than one float tuber suddenly found himself crashing into a pile of deadfall as his fish streaked downstream. Use your flippers or paddles to punch off such obstacles if you find yourself coming close.

Pick a spot to finish the fight—find an eddy or some slack pocket water. You don't want to be moving in current when you're focused on landing your fish. Now an important accessory comes into play: the long-handled net. When you've got your fish in close, put the net into the water and hold the handle flush against the tube or pontoon. Lean the rod back behind you, over your shoulder, and lift the rod tip, either with your wrist, or by raising your arm and then cocking your wrist. Bring the fish over the mouth of the net, and raise the mesh. You'll have your arms spread about as wide as they can go at this point.

The Canoe 4

The guide paddled silently toward where the tarpon was feeding. Once within casting range, he positioned his canoe at an angle such that his client would have a clear back cast. Two casts—one false cast and then the delivery—put the fly in the feeding path of the big fish. The tarpon took it, the client set the hook, the water exploded, and the fight was on. A skilled paddler, the guide kept his client and the fish lined up with each other. When the big fish turned, the guide would turn with him; when the tarpon jumped, the guide would make a quick long paddle stroke toward the fish, to stop the tarpon from tightening the line and breaking off. The battle raged on as the great fish headed for the open sea, leaving the flats behind and luring the canoe and its occupants behind it.

This scenario was derived from *The Book of the Tarpon* by A.W. Dimock, first published in 1910. Dimock recorded scene after scene of catching tarpon from a canoe while a skilled friend paddled. Dimock had tarpon land on him, capsize his canoe, and was also one of the first anglers to catch one of those great silver fish on the fly. Mr. Dimock's adventures were an elegant testament as to what a skilled angler and a skilled paddler can do in a canoe.

Fly-fishing and canoes have been together for hundreds of years. When rivers ran through this country, undammed and unmolested, the canoe was an important form of transportation in the exploration of our continent. In what other craft could you load enough camping gear for a two-week trip and still be able to fish from it?

While the canoe might be a more difficult craft to master, it has advantages over a kayak. In a canoe not only will you will have better access to your gear, you'll be able to carry more of it. One big advantage of the canoe is that waders or wetsuits are an option, not a necessity. Canoes are also warmer than kayaks, and—with knowledge, caution, and waterproof shoes or boots—you can stay dry in regular clothing.

The canoe, useful for eons in navigating waterways, is just as useful today to the angler.

In order to enjoy the fishing opportunities the canoe has to offer, you will need to learn some basic paddling skills. Based on my experience, it's a whole lot easier to learn how to paddle a canoe then it is learning to cast a fly rod. You may even be able to take a paddling class at the same store you took a casting class.

Let's start with canoe selection. Longer crafts, usually requiring two paddlers, will track better and give you more speed. Shorter canoes will give you less speed but more paddle sensitivity. The wider a craft, the more stable it is; the narrower a craft, the faster it is. For a fishing craft, you'll want a good compromise. The first thing you'll notice when you look in a canoe catalog is that they're listed in categories such as recreation, touring, whitewater, and expedition; the list can go on. Here are some of the different types of canoes.

Tandem canoes will be the most practical choice for multiple users. You can take others fishing with you to share the paddling chores as well as the fishing, and will have enough room to store gear for a week-long river trip. Or, you can simply take your spouse for a canoe ride down the river (which, incidentally, could be a good excuse to use to buy the canoe in the first place). The first thing you'll learn when paddling solo in a tandem for the first time is when you sit in the stern seat, the bow will rise up. When this happens the canoe will not track as well, and you'll waste energy with the extra strokes you'll need to keep it on track. On tandem models the bow seats are located closer to the center than the stern seat. It is the bow seat which will be the best location for a fly fisher paddling solo in a tandem model. To keep the bow down and your canoe's hull flat on the water so it will maneuver properly, you'll need some weight in the front. In the paddling community this is called "trimming" your canoe. When I trim my tandem canoe for solo fishing trips I use a cold box full of ice and goodies I'll need for the day, and a hard-shell waterproof

The Wenonah Vagabond pictured here is my own personal craft, which I paddle with a kayak paddle as well as a canoe paddle.

A solo canoe can be the craft for the spur-of-the-moment fisherman who wants to get in a couple of hours of early morning fishing before his day begins, or after it ends.

Pelican case for anything I don't want to get wet. If you plan to do a lot of solo fishing and your choice is a tandem canoe, try to keep the length under 16 feet.

Recreation canoes, though wider than tandems, do not have the performance features of the narrower touring models, but their stability and versatility make them a better choice for the fly fisherman new to the sport of paddling.

Touring canoes are designed for paddle sensitivity and speed. Again, touring canoes are narrower than recreation canoes, initial stability is reduced, and secondary stability is enhanced. This class of canoe is versatile in a variety of water conditions, and a good choice for a fisherman with some paddling experience.

Solo canoes are designed with the seat in its center, where you'll have the most control and power with your paddle stroke. My 43-pound, 14-foot and 5-inch Wenonah Vagabond solo is a craft I can load or unload to/from the roof of my vehicle in a matter of minutes. I can carry it with rods, paddle and gear secured over my shoulder when I need to portage or to simply launch. In my view, the solo canoe is the unsung hero of the paddling and fishing world.

For paddling fishermen, particularly fly fishermen, recreation and touring canoes will be the most efficient and safest choice.

The Wenonah Vagabond in the picture is my own personal craft, which paddles with a kayak paddle as well as a canoe paddle.

A solo canoe can be the craft for spur-of-the-moment fishermen who want to get in a couple of hours of early morning fishing before their day begins or after it ends.

Some people think paddling skills come with the purchase or rental of a paddling craft, but unfortunately for some, that train of thought has been fatal. As an experienced paddling fisherman, I do seminars at numerous events where kayak and canoe shops set up crafts at a local river or lake, and for a small fee let members of the public try out their canoes and kayaks. It is at these events where one can often witness unskilled individuals wreaking havoc. In one case I observed a couple sit down in a canoe for the first time, while a young salesman assisted them by holding the canoe until they were seated. The couple, not knowing any better, sat on one side rather than the center of the seat. The salesman, who had no experience other than selling canoes and kayaks, gave them a shove before I could yell a warning. Before you could say *paddle* we were looking at the bottom of their canoe. They didn't go two feet before they tipped over, because all their weight was on one side. In a canoe, always remember: low and center. Position yourself in the middle of your seat and keep as low a profile as you possibly can.

Canoes or kayaks are not dangerous, but paddling without proper knowledge can be. A day on the water with a good instructor will take substantial time off your learning curve, and have you well prepared for a safe paddling trip. Next to a good instructor, time on the water will be your best teacher. Learning your paddling strokes can be just as much fun as learning to cast.

Canoes can be paddled in all waters, depending on your skills. For safety's sake, it's imperative to know your skills and know your waters. Ponds are probably the simplest—what could be better than driving out to your favorite pond, putting your canoe in the water, paddling out in the middle of the pond, anchoring, sitting back relaxing, and casting a line till dark?

Canoes can be excellent for exploring many lakes. Paddling to the headwaters; working the shoreline, drop-offs, or structures; or simply being on open water can make paddling a canoe a wonderful experience. Keep a close eye on the weather, however, as strong unexpected winds can make open-water paddling in a canoe a hellish nightmare.

Rivers are where the canoe really shines. It can be a convenient vessel, powered by the strength of the river's current and skillful paddling strokes. The canoe can be loaded up for anywhere from a day to a couple of weeks on the river. While the elected paddler paddles, the angler can cast to pockets, riffles, and rises. To fish an area more thoroughly, you can anchor the canoe, or beach it and get out if you're in shallow waters. To go river fishing in a craft that has no need of fuel or batteries for power, in my mind the canoe is hard to beat.

Ocean angling is easily within the realm of possibilities as well. A.W. Dimock was casting a line from a canoe on Florida waters in the late 1800s, and you'll still find fishermen today poling after redfish and sea trout on the flats of Padre Island in Texas; chasing stripers and bluefish in estuaries along the East Coast; or casting lines to bonito, rock bass, and halibut in bays on the West Coast in a craft that's been around for centuries. You can still find guides along the Florida Coast that paddle their clients to within casting range of tarpons, in canoes. Whatever area of salt water you chose, the canoe is an able craft; just make sure you're an able paddler whatever craft you select for salt water. It's also prudent to paddle with a buddy, as two heads are not only better than one—they're safer.

As discussed for lake use, the canoe—for all its virtues—is highly susceptible to wind. When strong gusts blow, particularly out on open waters, paddling back to shore can be a real chore, even dangerous. I recall one day when I was assisting on a guided canoe trip on Millerton Lake, my home water in California. There was a wintry wind on the lake that day, and everyone was paddling hard to stay on course. I heard a yell, and turning around I saw them, a mother and son hanging on for dear life while their canoe was being blown across the lake. They were rescued, from what could have been a disastrous situation, by a couple of kayakers who were tagging along for the

The Fishin' Buddy is the perfect fish-finding companion for the canoeing angler.

tour. If it's a strong windy day on your favorite large body of water, salt or fresh, it's a good time to stay home and tie flies.

There are a number of considerations to keep in mind when rigging your canoe. These craft can carry more gear then any of the others covered in this book. You'll definitely have a lot more room to exercise your creativity; perhaps too much. The old saying "a place for everything and everything in its place" is particularly applicable. In a sixteen-foot canoe (my preferred length) there's room enough for two fly fishers, their gear, and enough camping gear for a week or more. And when it comes to rigging a canoe as a fishing craft, it's relatively simple.

Personal flotation devices are probably the first items to consider. Canoes do not tip over; people tip them over. When that happens, they should be wearing their life jackets.

Fish finders are a great asset in locating fish, but a transducer for a console model, installed on the floorboard of a canoe, would be exposed to kicks and bumps that could easily knock it loose, rendering it useless for the rest of the excursion. As I'm serious about my fishing, I've really come to depend on my fish finders, and the Fishin' Buddy is one of the best choices. This compact, easy-to-use unit with a highly adaptable clamp has worked well for me. Just remember to take it out of the clamp before you paddle into shallow water.

Paddle control is essential. Paddle clips are inexpensive and easy to use— I usually have two or three paddles in my canoe; the one I'm using and the others stored in the set up previously mentioned or in clips. Leashes can be useful to keep the paddles from getting lost, but in a canoe I would rather have an extra paddle handy than one on a leash. From past experience, a leash is easily tangled with a fly line, but some people use the leashes with little complaint.

A long-handled net or a Boga-Grip is the safest way to go for when

Canoe anchor system

you need to get a better handle on that big fish you finally wrestled boatside; you don't want to be leaning over the side of your canoe. And don't be shy about using all that room for whatever dry bags or cases (like those by Pelican) you'll need.

Anchor systems for a canoe need not be complicated. With the availability of commercially made anchor setups like the Scotty Anchor Lock for small boats, or my homemade one of ash wood and anchor hardware, there's no reason not to avail yourself of an appropriate system. The anchor pulley and clamp works the same for either my or Scotty's setup. Simply pull up at an angle to drop or pull up the anchor. All you have to do to use the brake is release your grip on the rope. Installation is easy; all one need do is to clamp them to the handle area on the canoe's stern.

Whenever you are paddling with a fishing buddy, whichever of you is at the bow casting must always be aware of the paddler. Never cast over him or her on either the forward or back cast. The safest way for two in a canoe is to have one fishing while one is paddling; the one who is fishing should straddle his seat, standing if he's confident in his balance, and sitting if not. From this position, he will be facing the side of the canoe. This maximizes the safety of the paddler, and makes the canoe its most efficient for fishing purposes. With paddler and fishermen working together in harmony, each knowing the other's skills, it will be paddle fishing at its best. Seated in the stern of the canoe, a paddler with quiet strokes can position the canoe to within a fifty-foot cast of those sipping trout, or a sixty-foot cast of tailing tarpon. The rest will be up to the fly fisher in the bow. Doing your casting and catching off

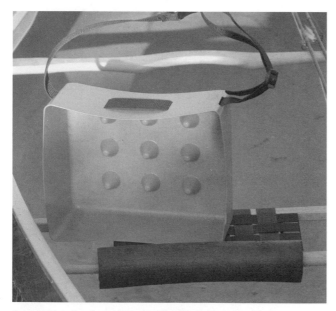

A stripping basket when fly fishing in a canoe can mean the difference between organized pleasure and chaotic frustration.

the side of the canoe will also allow the paddler to net (or BogaGrip) your fish for you.

On a river, the paddler can guide the canoe down the middle of the flow, holding the course while the fly fisher casts into pockets or coves along the bank on both sides of the river. A solo paddler with an anchor setup on his canoe can also fish a river, but his progress will be considerably slower as he will have to lower anchor every time he wants to cast.

Can you fly fish when you're solo in a canoe without an anchor? Yes. . . as long as there's no wind. One anchorless fishing trip was all it took to demonstrate this to me. It was a nice, sunny day in the middle of April; I was on the water by 9:00 a.m. that morning. It was Pine Flat Lake, a beautiful mountain lake about an hour's drive from my home in Fresno, California. The lake was like a mirror, with no winds whatsoever. Within a half hour on the water, I'd caught two fourteen-inch rainbow trout and about a three-pound largemouth bass. The fishing continued pleasantly for another hour or so. About eleven o'clock, the wind came, and after that it was pure hell and frustration. I put the stern of the canoe and my back to the wind. On my next cast, the line landed in a pile on the water. My second cast almost pierced my ear (for a second time). As long as this kept up, my canoe was highly susceptible to the wind, and without an anchor was moving constantly. In a canoe, you cannot paddle and cast at the same time.

As a fishing guide, my job is to be the paddler in the back seat (stern) of the

Canoe paddles come with bent shafts (great for canoe racing and long-distance or flat water paddling) or straight shafts (great for everything else).

The pear grip (right) gives you a more relaxed grip, for flat water. The T grip (left) provides you with a firm grip, great for rough water paddling.

Standard hold for a canoe paddle.

canoe, paddling my clients to within casting distance of fish while they cast from the bow. From the stern of my canoe, I can position the craft on the desired spot and hold it with a positioning stroke. When one paddles while the other is fishing, the canoe can be one of the most effective fishing crafts on the water.

Sometimes it might seem awkward handling the fly line while in a canoe, but I was delighted to discover that I could use one of my favorite accessories, the stripping baskets. I've used the Orvis stripping basket for years, and when I took my stripping basket along on my first fishing trip in a canoe, I found that it solved my line problem. It also works out great for those times when you anchor the canoe, and get out to fish. You can make your own stripping basket, but I like the Orvis model's safety belt and quick-release buckle.

The forward or power stroke is the mainstay of a canoeist's paddling repertoire. It begins by extending the paddle forward into the water, pulling it back while pushing with the other hand, and a good follow-through.

Need to move sideways? The draw stroke is just the ticket.

One last word on solo canoeing. Under these conditions, trolling a fly can be a handy technique. You can have your rod in a rod holder, which is the safest, or leaning against the rail or seat (where it had better be leashed).

The canoe paddle is the tool of self-propulsion. Your hand on the handle will be the control hand, and the one on the blade your power hand. Sitting in your canoe, extend your paddle forward and into the water just a bit past the blade. With the blade pointed down, keep your stroke as close as possible to the side of your canoe. Pull back with your power hand and push forward with your control hand and you will propel yourself forward across the water. This, the forward or power stroke, will be your most important tool. Think of your paddling know-how as a tree of knowledge. A good forward or power stroke will be the trunk of your tree, and your other paddling strokes its limbs. If the trunk is strong, the limbs will also be.

For those times when you need to move your canoe sideways, the draw stroke comes into play. Begin by holding your paddle parallel to your hip. With your hand on the grip, submerge the paddle in the water a little past the blade. Begin the stroke by pushing the blade away from your hip, edge of blade first.

The J-stroke is extremely useful as well. You're paddling on the right; your canoe veers to the left. A properly executed J-stroke will keep your craft tracking straight. Begin with a good forward stroke. At the end of the forward stroke turn your paddle on its edge.

(You know you're doing the J correctly if your control hand is positioned thumbs down.)

An accomplished canoeist uses a J stroke often. Begin with a good forward stroke; at the end of the forward stroke turn the paddle on its edge.

You know you're doing it correctly if your control hand is positioned thumb down.

Swing your blade out, and then lift it out of the water.

A well-executed J-stroke takes time and practice, and used properly it will save time and energy.

FISHING TACTICS

Targeting Fish in Current, Rivers, or Streams

The techniques I'm about to share with you are best suited for a beginning paddler in a 36-inch wide, 14- to 15-feet long standard recreation canoe. A good anchor system (see page 29) is essential for fishing fast moving water from a canoe, particularly if you're the only one in the craft.

If you've ever fished with a guide in a drift boat, and you've cast to an obviously fishy spot without a strike, sometimes the guide will pull out of the main current, row back upstream through a seam of slower water, and set you up for a second shot at the lie.

You can very easily do the same for yourself while fishing from a canoe in a stream or river: Pick your target, make your cast, throw a mend, and anticipate the strike. You can work three targets in succession, and then set the rod down, with the fly in the keeper, and make a U-turn back upstream to try the run again. (I don't let my fly drag in the water while moving; some people say this might work to hook a fish, but in my experience, all I do is hook branches and rocks.)

Your approach to a fish should always be quartering downstream at a slight angle. You don't want to get any more broadside in the water. As you approach a fishy spot, backpaddle to give yourself a chance to observe the location. If you happen to see a group of fish feeding—perhaps there's a blue-winged olive hatch—or you want to take your time and cast to both banks and downstream, this is a case for using your anchor.

When I drop anchor in moving water, I let it go straight down to the bottom. Then I let my canoe drift a few feet to secure the anchor. Because my anchor setup is on the stern of my craft, the current will hold my canoe in place and keep the bow pointing downstream. I can now work the water in front of me, the banks on either side of me, or repeatedly cast to a group of feeding fish. Never cast over the anchor, or the stern. Losing one good fish because it wrapped my line around the anchor rope and broke off was enough for me.

There's a limit to what kind of current in which you can anchor. A stream that's running high with a strong current can be dicey in an anchored kayak. If you hook a big fish and it runs hard left or right, you'll find that as you move in the kayak, the current will push pretty hard against the sides, making for an unstable situation.

Quick casting and deft mending are necessary skills for casting to fish from a canoe that's moving in the current. If you cast to slower water around a rock, or along a bubble line in an eddy, you'll need to strip and mend to keep a reasonably direct, slack-free connection to your fly.

Covering Water and Prospecting for Fish

The use of an anchor isn't always necessary when fishing solo in a canoe. As you drift down a river or along the shore of a reservoir you'll have a better vantage point than any of the other crafts in this book because of how high you sit. Holding your course can be as simple as a quick one-arm brace stroke. To perform a one-arm stroke, brace the shaft of the paddle against your forearm, with the handle in the bend of your arm.

Let's say that you see some surface activity ahead, off to the right. You put down your paddle and pick up the rod and make a cast. A good fish follows your fly but doesn't hit. You need to back up for another cast.

Use a one-arm backwards stroke on the left side of your canoe to gain some distance upstream, and ready another cast as you put your paddle down against the thwart (one of the wooden braces that connect the sides of the canoe) and let the cast go as the current again picks you up.

You'll also be able to hold your course along the water's edge without putting your rod down by using the one-arm stroke. As I mentioned before, a stripping basket can be an excellent accessory in a canoe. It will give you something you'll desperately need: a place to store your line as you cast. You can either wear the basket or keep it down on the hull between your feet.

FIGHTING AND LANDING LARGER FISH

O.k.—you've connected with the fish of a lifetime and the fight is on.

You're able to pull it away from the cover, but then the fish turns and heads for new cover. . .and comes rapidly toward your canoe. Extend your rod tip forward over the bow as far as you can, giving the line and the fish enough clearance to swim under the canoe without catastrophe.

Now the battle rages on the other side of your canoe and in the middle of the river. The fish heads downriver with you in tow. Your rod tip and the bow are pointing in the direction of the fish is headed. You'll need to slow the fish down a bit. Put a proper, even bend in the rod and lean it toward the closest bank, thus turning the fish into slower, more shallow water where you can pick a spot to land the fish. You might go through this process several times as the fish runs, jumps, and bulldogs down on the bottom, depending upon the fighting habits of the species. The tough part is keeping one eye on where the current is taking you and not becoming wholly absorbed in the fight.

Once you are able to steer the fish into shallower water, start using your long-handled net like a paddle, with the handle of the net positioned against your arm as you would a paddle. As you hold your rod in one hand, line tightly gripped against the handle with your fingers, execute a brief one arm stroke with the other, causing the canoe to angle just a bit, slowing the fish down, almost as if your were tightening the drag (the fish is now up against the rod pressure and the weight of the canoe).

Finally, when you've fought to within netting range of the fish, comes the moment when you must kneel down on the hull (I keep a 3x3 piece of foam padding for this) to maintain control and ward against a possible capsize. As I extend the net under the fish and lift on the left side of my craft, I lean toward the right side, raising the rod in my right hand. In doing so I keep the canoe balanced. Lay down the rod as you bring the fish into the boat.

The canoe is an adventurous and challenging craft, and I will never be without one. However, I found the ocean somewhat intimidating when paddling in its waters, so my search was not quite over.

The Kayak

Since I started paddling and casting from a kayak, I've caught all manner of fish, from rock bass along the jetties of Dana Point in San Diego, to three-foot lingcod in the kelp beds in front of the Santa Cruz Boardwalk. Best of all, the kayak has allowed me to effectively fish my dream waters, the California Delta. The same craft that people in-

digenous to the Arctic and other waters used for survival has allowed many an angler to fish waters they never could before.

Well over a thousand years ago, in the Arctic and other waters, Inuit, Aleutian, and other native peoples established the kayak as a seagoing craft for fishing and hunting. The same factors causing

The kayak.

the success of this craft established centuries ago undoubtedly come into play today, when you'll find kayak anglers a common sight in the waters off the coast of the Pacific and Atlantic Oceans, as well as other waters of the world. For the modern-day kayak anglers, the ocean and the fish that swim in it can be their great adventure, their own personal frontier.

While salt water is one frontier for the 'yak angler, fresh water is another. Between the Atlantic and the Pacific Oceans there are lakes and rivers just waiting to be explored. Properly rigged and handled, the kayak can be your magic carpet to fish that swim in all waters.

Out of all the crafts covered in this book, you may well think the kayak the most difficult craft from which to learn to cast a fly line. Yet the truth is, and I'm talking about a sit-on-top kayak when I say this, it's the easiest. With a few basic strokes and casts, a little bit of practice, and a properly rigged kayak, I've had fly-fishing clients who'd never paddled before manage a pretty good day of fishing, after an hour of instruction. . . and it's not because I'm an outstanding instructor.

Most fishermen shopping for their first kayak will likely go to a kayak shop. When this happens, two different individuals will meet: the fisherman and the kayak salesman, two different people from two different worlds. Unfortunately, much of the time neither knows anything about the other's world. It's my hope that this book will help to bring those two worlds together.

What should you, as fishermen—particularly if you've never paddled before—be looking for when you buy your first kayak? First on the list should be comfort. Casting or paddling, you'll be sitting while you do it. There are several brands of seats on the market; look for one that has padding and is easily adjustable. A fisherman needs a good, comfortable seat in his kayak if he's going to paddle to that hot spot, and then back again at the end of the day.

Stability is next. When you try out a kayak for fishing, paddle it until you're confident in its stability. Then cast from it. I have a saying for beginning 'yak fishermen when it come to feeling unstable in their craft: "when in doubt, straddle." In other words, stick those feet in the water and you'll have instant outriggers.

After comfort and stability, you should be thinking about handling or paddle response. Just because a kayak is stable doesn't necessarily mean it's going to paddle well, because stable usually means slower. Wider 'yaks are more stable than narrow ones. Longer kayaks will track better and give you more speed, whereas shorter kayaks can be more sensitive to the paddle.

Last but not least is the layout for rigging. You should make sure the layout of your intended 'yak lends itself to your needs. You want to be able to install rod holders out of the way of your paddle stroke. You'll also want an area for a fish finder, preferably on the console. I have found that personally rigging your kayak is a big part of kayak fishing.

While I have a definite preference for sit-on-top kayaks for fishing, here are some descriptions of the different kayaks available.

Touring or sea kayaks are as close to "true" kayaks as you're going to get. The width of these varies from 21 inches to as narrow as 17 inches. They have a small cockpit into which the paddler has to slide. You will also have to add a skirt to your wardrobe—a spray skirt, actually. A spray skirt is a waterproof cover designed to attach to the coaming (cockpit rim) of the kayak and your body. The purpose of the spray skirt is to keep paddle drips, rain and large dumping waves out of your kayak. The skirt seals off the cockpit and traps in warm air, making it very useful during cooler weather. (Unfortunately, it does the same during the summer.)

I bought a touring kayak for the sake of paddling efficiently, and here's what I discovered: (1) If it isn't leashed, don't set it down on the decks of a sea kayak, because it will slide right off. (2) Don't depend too much on being able to turn around to get something on the deck behind you—due to the small cockpit of a touring 'yak, your maneuverability is very limited. (3) I don't do the Eskimo roll, and it's the last thing I'd want to do in a fully rigged fishing 'yak. (The Eskimo roll is the maneuver in which a kayak spins completely around, along its long axis, submerging the paddler. A skilled operator under the right conditions can continue the spin until the craft rights itself, leaving him little the worse for wear other than a brief dunking.)

Recreational kayaks have a larger cockpit; most are around 58 inches in length, compared to a sea kayak's 30-inch average. You can get a spray skirt for a recreational model, but they look more like a spray dress and I wouldn't want to have to swim in one. They also have what they call a mini skirt that just covers half the cockpit and it makes a good stripping apron. In calmer waters a spray skirt will not be necessary; however, any time there is any kind of chop or wave action going on, the large cockpit will enable them to take on water. If they fill up, they'll weigh five times what they did when they were empty.

Managers of some lakes do not allow body contact with the water, meaning no float tubes, pontoon boats, or sit-on-top kayaks, but they do allow those that one sits inside. For cold winter waters or for a second kayak, a recreational kayak isn't a bad choice. It's important to remember to paddle a recreation yak in calm waters only, however.

For fishermen wanting to use a kayak for a fishing platform, sit-on-top models are the way to go. The primary reasons are the crafts' stability, easy access, plenty of room for storage (beneath the hatches and on top for rod holders and other gear), and the best of all—they're safer for fishermen. In a kayak set up for fly fishing, the last thing I would want to do is the Eskimo roll. If you capsize in a sit-on-top kayak, you simply climb up on the bottom of the kayak, grab the handle on the side with both hands, and pull up while you push down with both knees on the other side. Once this procedure has been applied, you should be ready to get back to your fishing. . . providing you had everything waterproofed or at least leashed down. At the very least, a capsize will cause the loss of tackle, gear, and anything else that isn't tied down. In my opinion, the safest choice is a sit-on-top.

For years, SOTs were more or less just water toys; they had little speed and

Recreational kayak

about as much paddling sensitivity as a log. (I've actually paddled a log down a river, so I speak from experience.) In an SOT, entrance or exit is simple—you go in butt first, feet last, and you get out feet first, butt last. You can turn around, and hang your legs over the side for easy access to your rear hatch or fishing crate, or simply to fish.

This Wilderness system 120 is a good example of what I consider to be a properly rigged kayak, with a convenient tank well—perfect for storing cold boxes and of course fishing crates.

My choice is a kayak with an open well (positioned on the deck in front of the paddler) or tank well (positioned behind; so called because of its convenience for divers' tanks). The latter is a handy opened space in the back of most SOT kayaks for storage, perfect for storing cold boxes and of course fishing crates.

What's the best length for a fishing kayak? SOTs are available from eight to seventeen feet. For big waters like the ocean, large freshwater reservoirs, or rivers—when I know I'll be dealing with strong winds—my choice is a sixteen-footer. For smaller rivers, or anywhere I'd have to make a fast turn to dodge a boulder, navigate a sharp river bend, or just simply fishing on a small pond, I prefer a 12-foot craft. If your budget or space can't handle two kayaks, a good compromise is a 14-foot craft.

For the fly caster who doesn't have the room to store a kayak or the right vehicle to transport it to the water, 'yak fishing can still be attainable. The convenience of having a fishing craft you can keep in a bag small enough to take on a plane as luggage, unbag it at your fishing destination, inflate it, and go fishing just isn't available to pontoon and float tube owners. We're talking about inflatable kayaks. Inflatable 'yaks can be rigged up in a manner somewhat similar to plastic ones, and they paddle quite well. You will need a longer paddle, say 240 cm, as inflatables are a bit wider and your paddle

Inflatable kayaks can go from this (left) neatly folded stack to this (right) completely navigable craft.

Kayak paddles are available in a variety of shapes and styles. Pictured here are (from top to bottom) the Sawyer Greenland paddle, Western-style touring paddle, Aqua Bound touring paddle, low-end power blade, and high-end power blade.

handle will need a longer reach. The one down side to inflatables, however, is that they are more vulnerable to wind.

The kayak paddle is unique among those tools of propulsion covered in this book. The double-bladed design—having a blade on both ends of the shaft—can provide a level of control not possible in the other crafts in this book. Proper hand placement for the Western-style kayak paddle is both hands on the shaft at least eight inches from the blades. Hold the paddle so that the edge of the blades lines up with your knuckles. The convex side of the blade should be pointing forward. With the blade pointed down, keep your stroke as close as possible to the side of your 'yak. Extend your paddle forward and into the water just a bit past the blade, and pull back with your power hand while pushing forward with your control hand and you will propel your self forward across the water using the power stroke in a kayak.

Depending on the materials from which a paddle is made, you can spend anywhere from $80 to $400. Materials are not the only variable; another is blade shape. The power blade is shaped like a cupped hand, allowing it to grab a lot of water and propel you across the water quickly. You can use the power blade for most applications, except for paddling a long distance as the payment for all the power is increased exertion.

The touring blade is a bit narrower and longer then the power blade; it will grab less water, therefore reducing strain on the muscles. With practice, you can paddle painlessly with it over miles of water.

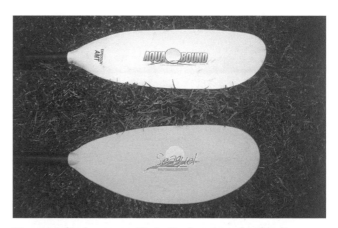

More detail of a power blade (top) and touring blade.

One morning several decades ago, my family and I were camping on Belton Lake, a popular reservoir located in my home state of Texas. Our camp was right by the water. The first one to rise from bed that morning, I grabbed the inflated air mattress I'd been using to sleep on, and headed for the lake. Wading out a few feet, I placed the mattress on the water. Laying down on the mattress, I spread my arms out like wings, and using my hands for paddles I flew across the water. It was the most exciting thing to ever happen to a nine-year-old boy. I spent the day paddling all around the cove near our campsite.

For me it was my first self-propelled experience; this was the way I would always want to travel

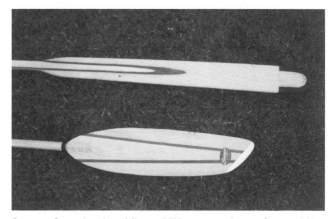

Sawyer Greenland paddle and Western-style touring paddle.

across the water. It was fantastic, I thought—until I woke up the next morning and felt the pain in my arms. I remember that feeling of flying over the water, propelled by the strength of my arms, to this day. Every time I sit down in a kayak, pick up my paddle, and propel myself across the water, I relive that experience. . . minus the pain.

The similarity between that seminal event and the double-bladed kayak paddle is one of the main reasons I am attracted to this craft. It's important to realize that your paddle is no small matter; it is the steering wheel and not just an accessory.

There are almost as many different paddle strokes for the kayaker as there are fly casts. Fortunately, you only need to learn a few of either to be an effective paddling fishermen. It is therefore prudent to choose your paddle as carefully as you did your fly rod or your craft. Do not buy the cheapest paddle you can find. Many times I've seen an individual paddling a kayak worth a few hundred dollars using a paddle worth a few bucks. You should not buy a kayak without trying it out first; the same goes for your paddle. Any reputable kayak shop will rent you a kayak and a paddle so you can try them out. Kayak shops and paddling associations will also have "paddle days" on local waters, where suppliers will bring many different brands and types of kayaks, paddles, canoes, PFD's, and other accessories.

A Paddlefest is a great opportunity to learn about kayaks, as well as try some models out.

If you're new to kayaking and would like to know more, it's a good idea to attend a local Paddlefest, which is essentially a paddling carnival. Along with sporting just about every make of kayak and canoe, it is likely to include some instructional classes, as well as appearances by some of the world's best paddlers. Attend one of these events, and you'll gain paddling knowledge as well as some useful data toward your decision on which craft and paddle will work best for you.

Taking a basic paddling class will make your time on the water a whole lot easier. It takes a significant chunk of time off your learning curve and keeps you from having any bad kayak experiences. Further, I highly recommend that you make a few trips to the water before you do any fishing, in order to get comfortable in your kayak, improve your balance, and solidify your paddling skills.

Once you do get a basic paddling class out of the way, it's worth considering a second, more advanced, class that will prepare you for those bad experiences when they do happen. Most reputable kayak shops will have such a class—one that will teach you to read the water as well as paddle in it, along with how to get back in your kayak when you fall out of it, or help someone else when they do.

THE OTHER HALF OF INUIT GENIUS

It's been a few years now since I started casting and paddling. Every kind of paddle imaginable has propelled my kayak to the waters I fish: those with blades made of polythalamide, Kevlar, or fiberglass on the ends of shafts made up of everything from aluminum to carbon—highly efficient but cold to the touch. Another option, and my overall choice of paddle, is the instrument of self-propulsion used by the Inuit to power the first kayak, known in modern time as the Greenland or Inuit paddle. The shaft length of the Greenland paddle isn't much wider then a typical man's waist. The rest of the paddle is all blade, which is little more than three or four inches wide at best.

I am constantly looking for easier ways to combine fishing and kayaking, and this style of paddling suits me well. When I'm fishing, the paddle is lying right across my lap, up against my stomach, so that I'll be ready for any paddling or fishing situation. Every time I grabbed for my Western paddle—for situations such as repositioning myself because I floated away from a hot spot, or I've hooked a good-size fish and I've got to back him out of heavy cover with a single-armed stroke—I would have to look down and make sure the blade was lined up with my knuckles, and that the convex side of the paddle was pointing forward. It was a bit too much.

The width of the Western-style blade is around six to seven inches. A paddle stroke with this tool is going to be slower, because of the amount of water the more-widely-concave blade grabs. The flat, narrow, Greenland blade will cut through the water much faster (particularly if the blade is at an angle), because it grabs less water. You hold the paddle where the shaft meets the blades, with the thumb and index finger on the shaft and the remaining fingers on the blade. Once this grasp is established in your mind, it will be all but impossible to grab the Greenland paddle incorrectly.

Once you've acquired some basic paddle skills, such as the forward/back, turning, and bracing strokes, as well as how to make your abdomen and shoulder muscles participate as well as your arm muscles, you'll be flying across water. Paddling a kayak is also great exercise for the upper body, and proper paddling can make a bad back better. I'm as flatfooted as they come, and for many people that can mean a bad lower back. For me, paddling a kayak has put an end to back pain. . . and those really boring exercises.

Once you go this route, it might be wise to be prepared for some (what we hope will be) good-natured harassment from those who have no idea of its effectiveness in the water. I've heard things like, "would you like for us to take up a collection so you can buy a paddle?" and "stop using that two-by-four" or "when are you going to stop using that toothpick and get a real paddle?"

But I've also heard, from the same mouths after seeing me paddle up

The author demonstrating how to hold the Greenland paddle properly.

a river or through the surf, "not bad for someone using a toothpick." I've converted many a non-believer to a believer by simply letting them try the Greenland paddle.

A couple of years ago I served as the kayak pond director for the International Sportsmen Exposition here on the West Coast. I spoke on kayak fishing and kayaking in general, and demonstrated paddling and fishing techniques in the small exhibition pond they had provided. After each talk, I would encourage members of the audience to paddle a kayak around the pond, and even try casting from one. Most of them were paddling a kayak for the first time. I would help each brave soul up the ladder and into the kayak (most of the kayaks were sit-on-top models). Once they were comfortably in the kayak, I would hand them a Greenland paddle. All I would do was show them how to hold it, and tell them to do what came naturally—nothing else. They would awkwardly paddle around the pool for a few minutes, until they got comfortable. Next thing you know, their strokes got smoother and the kayak they were paddling was moving gracefully around the pond, while a look of confidence would grow over their face. It provided yet more evidence of what I already knew—the Greenland paddle brings out one's natural abilities.

Before I begin with the basic strokes, let me say this. I've had no formal training with the Greenland paddle. The knowledge I'm about to share with you comes from time—trial and error on the water and a generous sharing of knowledge from a wonderful website called Qaannat Kattuffiat (www.qajaqusa.org)

Qaannat Kattuffiat, the Greenland Kayaking Association, is a Greenland-based organization that is dedicated to keeping the traditional kayaking skills of Greenland alive.

I would like to acknowledge and thank two individuals for sharing their knowledge in articles on the Qaannat Kattuffiat website: the first—Greenland Style Paddling: An Overview—by Brian Day and the second—Maligiaq Makes Waves on his U.S. Visit—by the late John Heath. The knowledge from their articles made it easy for me to learn the basics of Greenland paddling on the water.

As far as I know there aren't any instructors in the United States who teach Greenland kayaking or paddling.

Knowing your strokes while kayaking is at least as important as with any other craft, and the forward stroke will be your most important. Look at your paddling know-how as a tree of knowledge. Properly done, a good forward stroke will be the trunk of your tree, and your other paddling strokes the limbs. If the trunk is strong, the limbs will also be.

For your learning curve I have included Western paddling instructional images as well as Greenland.

Start on the water in a sit-on-top model. Your seat and thigh braces should be adjusted so that you're comfortable, and your paddle is resting across your lap. Keeping your elbows low and rigid, hold the paddle at a horizontal position; lift it up no higher than your chest. When you make your first stroke, brace firmly with your right knee against your thigh brace or push on your right footrest. Your paddle stroke shouldn't be more than 14–20 inches in length, and it should begin at your knee and end at your hip. With this technique you will be able to take faster, shorter strokes. The paddle blade shouldn't be more than ten inches under the surface at any time. Put the blade in the water parallel to the bow, rotating your torso as you do so.

Pull back with your pulling hand and push forward with the pushing hand. As you pull with your pulling hand, once again brace firmly with your knee against your thigh brace or push on your right footrest. Don't just use your arms, which are your smallest paddling muscles, as your main paddling force. Use your abdomen, back, and chest as

The kayaker's power stroke: undoubtedly the most important item for the user's tool kit.

well. In fact, it should be your torso that provides most of the power. (A good measure for proper use of the torso is to observe the zipper on your PFD—it will moving from side to side while you paddle.) Six to eight strokes will have you moving at a good clip across the water.

The forward stroke, performed properly with a Greenland paddle, is an-energy saving stroke that you can use to propel your craft across the waters for hours on end without fatigue or pain, and it will be just as useful to hold your position on your destination spot once you get there.

The stealth stroke is almost as useful, and can be critical under some circumstances. If you gripped the paddled as described earlier, it tilted the top edge of the paddle forward at an angle of 30 degrees or so, causing it to slice into the water at a slight angle as you began your stroke. Again, your stroke should end at the hip. If the angle is held throughout the stroke, returning as well as forward, the blade will also slice out of the water at the end of the stroke, resulting in a complete stroke that is essentially noise-free and minimally disturbing to

The power stroke, with the Greenland paddle (top) and Western paddle (bottom).

Brace stroke

the water. With practice, you will be able to use this to paddle silently within easy casting range of fish, or within convenient photography range of wildlife.

The turning stroke is a simple technique. If you want to turn right, put your right blade in the water—and brace firmly if you already have some forward momentum, or do a reverse stroke. Reverse this procedure, of course, for a left turn. You should practice your bracing until it's second nature. Brace strokes are the ones that will help you avoid a boulder in the middle of a fast-moving river, or make that sharp turn caused by a bend in the river.

To stop, use short, repeated left and right braces parallel with your hips; after the first two braces, push forward with the next two. And to move in reverse, it's a simple matter to simply paddle backwards. I still see new 'yakers in tight situations turn their whole rig around before they realized that all they have to do is paddle backwards.

The draw stroke is probably the easiest way to move your kayak sideways. Begin by holding your paddle vertically and parallel to your hip. With one blade pointing straight up—and the other completely submerged in the water a little past the blade—begin by pushing the blade away, edge first, as if you're cutting water from your hip. At the end of your stroke, turn your blade to the normal position and pull back the blade back to your hip. Avoid beginning the stroke by pushing the side of your blade out first, as it greatly increases the chances for a capsizing.

The sculling stroke is a good supporting, as well as a sideways, stroke. It's not a stroke I use in an SOT, but it's one upon which I rely for those times

The draw stroke, shown for the Greenland paddle (left) and Western paddle (right)

I'm in a sea kayak. While all good paddling takes practice, this stroke is likely to take more then the others. You begin as you would in preparation for a draw stroke, only you will be making a compressed figure-eight motion, at an angle that you can vary. As you make the figure eight, think of it as though you are spreading icing on a cake. You want the stroke to be angled enough such that your blade is always rising toward the surface. Using the sculling stroke, an experienced sea kayaker can put his kayak all the way over on its side without capsizing. It's worth mentioning, however, that this is not really something I'd want to do in an SOT rigged for fishing.

Paddle position bears some additional repetition. When I'm fishing, my paddle is laying across my lap ready for any situation. For example, a power-boat may come speeding by me while I'm fishing, causing a large wake. The waves from the wake—large enough to cause a capsizing, if the wake is big enough and the 'yaker isn't prepared—are going to hit my left side. I merely extend my paddle out a bit, lay the face of the blade down on the surface of the oncoming waves, and brace with the paddle and my left knee (we hope that the user is wearing thigh braces). If all goes well, I will merely surf sideways for a few feet; how many feet will depend on the size and speed of the craft that made the wake.

The bow stroke can put you sideways in one smooth motion.

To meet a wave or wake in more directed fashion, one can use the bow sweep stroke: Imagine that you are confronting the same wake as before. This time, however, you want to face the oncoming wave with your bow and not your side. (This is where the Greenland paddle shines.) Extend your paddle's blade in the water so that its face is against the right side of your bow. As a wave is coming in toward your left side, your left hand should be on the shaft, the right hand on the end of the other blade. One side sweep or stroke and your bow will be facing the wave. To completely reverse the direction of your kayak, begin a sweep stroke at the stern.

Concerning paddle length, I would say that size definitely matters. I have interviewed kayak shop owners and other kayakers, and the overall, most popular choice is 230 centimeters. Whitewater and some other paddlers often use a shorter paddle (say, 200 cm). For sea kayakers, 220 cm might be more appropriate. For all others—recreational, sit-on-top, anglers—the popular choice remains 230 cm. Sure, it's possible to get a longer stroke with a 240-cm paddle, but it will also require more effort into each stroke. . . which you will most definitely remember, when you are complaining about your sore muscles at the end of the day.

Earlier we discussed some of the different paddle styles available, but there's no reason not to take advantage of the multiplicity available. Think of the paddle as your steering wheel, the power blade your acceleration pedal, and the touring blade your cruise control—on those days when you have to paddle a few miles across a lake, to get to the headwaters where the river meets the lake. . . paddling down a river for a couple of days of fishing and camping. . . exploring a large body of calm flat water. It could be your home waters, or a three-day guided tour along the coast of the Pacific Ocean. Use your cruise control (the long, slender touring blade) for covering long distances. Use the power blade for those times when you want to fly across the water for the sheer joy of it, or when you've misjudged how far away those thunderheads are. It's always a good idea to have an extra paddle at all times, located within easy access on your kayak—one never knows how an unleashed paddle could get lost, far from the nearest shore or outpost of civilization.

Rudders are an interesting subject in the world of kayaks. There are two different camps on rudders, one positive and one negative. In the positive camp, people appreciate that they can simply put the rudder down and just paddle—a rudder can stop strong winds from ruining the day, and the boater won't have to correct his paddle stroke so much. For those kayakers who paddle long distances, a rudder can be a real energy saver. I tend to be part of this camp—when paddling along a shore with the wind at your back, casting your line to the structure the shore offers you, the rudder can keep your course straight with just a little bit of paddling. With practice, the rudder can be the kayak fishermen's friend.

The negative camp's position? With good paddling skills, you'll never need a rudder, which can get in the way of structure in shallow water.

I do agree that one does need to remember to pull the rudder up when paddling into shallow water, and that they're no substitute for good paddling skills. However, as a kayak fisherman, I realize there are times when paddling home after a long and tiring day that paddling a straight line can be just about all I can handle. If I paddled across a large lake to get to headwaters where the river feeds the lake, then paddle up that river, and spend the day engaged in some of the best striper and shad fishing you could ask for, then paddling back after such a day is when I love the rudder.

The rudder itself isn't really all that fragile, and yes it will come up if you paddle into water that is too shallow. Another consideration is that the footrests on top of the rudders have a tendency to pop out; sometimes even the whole track will come out. Beginning paddlers sometimes forget and push on both foot rests at the same time. They can sink, and I've had to replace a few.

The rudder can be a great asset to control the drift of the kayak, so your hands can be free to fish and do other things. One useful technique that I've found involves determining the direction of the wind and paddling into it, marking fish as I go. Once I've marked a reasonable amount of water, I'll turn my 'yak around putting my back to the wind. First I lower my rudder, and then drop the drift chute in the water attached to about eight feet of rope. The drift chute slows down the kayak to a snail's crawl, and I can then fish a good stretch of water with my hands free.

RIGGING YOUR KAYAK

When rigging your new kayak, the very first item to contemplate is the PFD (Personal Flotation Device). Out of all the crafts covered in this book, the kayak is undoubtedly the one in which this device is the most important.

Kayak fishing adventures can be sought in all waters—pursue them safely and wear your life jacket.

If you're serious about catching fish, then a fish finder is practically mandatory, and a console model is my first choice. There are times, however, such as when I am exploring new waters and I just have to have that side view, when I take along my Bottom Line Fishin' Buddy. The same adapter that holds the Fishin' Buddy on the float tube can be used for the kayak. Simply take the buckle off the longer strap, run the strap through one of the scupper holes, then put the buckle back on and tighten it up. Make sure it's tight or your fishfinder could swing under water. If you've installed rod holders—which I recommend very strongly, for holding rods as well as nets (or BogaGrips)—then these can be used as well.

Keeping your equipment secure is also important, which brings us to clips and leashes. A good paddle stroke ends at the hip, and with that thought in mind I installed my first clip a foot behind me and the second clip about eighteen inches behind that. Clips so positioned will not interfere with the paddling. (Most newer kayak designs do not require paddle clips.) Leashes also have their use; my fly rod is leashed to a screw eye, or its equivalent, on the 'yak's right side, and the paddle is similarly leashed to the left side.

Tackle bags and fly boxes need to be organized as well. My flies, of which there are a large variety, are stored in plastic Plano containers that are kept in a soft tackle bag, which in turn is stored in the hatch. I simply take the appropriate plastic container of flies out of the tackle bag and place it in the tank well, or the pocket on the back of my seat where it will be handy when needed.

If my fishing trip is going to be longer than a day, I use two large dry bags for extra clothing, sleeping bag, tent, and cooking utensils. I use two different size Pelican cases—the larger one carries all my photo gear for those times when I'm out for photos, and the smaller one carries my camera with one lens that I carry in my kayak at all times.

With a properly rigged kayak, you are organized, and all gear—anchor, fishfinder, rods, net, paddle, extra paddle, drink, sunscreen, camera—are accounted for. If your kayak is orderly, everything can be reachable and your sanity and temper will be kept in check.

Now we're ready for our first adventure in kayak fly fishing: rigging and customizing your 'yak, which need not be as labor intensive as it might sound. A fully rigged kayak should have a proper anchor setup, a fishfinder, and a fishing basket with holders for a net, a rolling pin anchor setup (to be further discussed), a small cooler, plus whatever other little odds and ends you might want to take. Additionally, there should be room to install rod holders and to store a tackle bag for easy access. With the right setup you'll be able to cover water quickly and fish all waters—ponds, lakes, rivers, and oceans. With experience you'll be able to catch any fish, from a bluegill to a bluefin tuna.

One of the hardest tasks any kayaker will ever have to do will be to drill a hole in their vessel. Make sure you have the right size drill bit, so the hole will be the right size, for whatever you're installing, be it a screw eye, rivet, or bolt. Always do a practice drill with a piece of scrap wood. If you do drill a hole in the wrong place, it's not the end of the world; a screw and a plastic or rubber washer will plug the hole.

Fly fishermen in particular should exercise forethought before they begin drilling holes in their kayaks. The behavior of fly line while it is being handled and cast must be uppermost in the customizer's mind while determining what changes are to be made. Good line control is always important but never more so than when fishing out of a kayak. You'll want to install rod holders or paddle clips on the deck behind you, not alongside where you're sitting in the cockpit and casting fly line. If these items are installed in this area, your fly line is far more likely to find these items and wrap around them, making you scream bad things. It's wise to first go out and do some paddling, so you'll know where the paddle blade winds up. Whatever you install, you will not want it to interfere with your paddle stroke (which, again, should never go past your hip). The repeated banging or catching of your paddle blade against a badly placed rod holder or paddle clip will make you crazy.

ACCESSORIES

Fish Finder or Depth Gauge. A fish finder is a piece of technology I embrace, and one piece of equipment you should have, as it will save you a lot of time on the water. I fish lakes, rivers, and bays, up and down the state of California. I love to explore new waters, and I would rather explore by paddling and observing, rather than blind casting. A good fish finder does just what the name says; it finds where the fish are and—just as important— where they are not. More than once I've spent time in areas that I thought looked really fishy, only to find after I started using a fish finder that they rarely held fish. In a paddle craft you don't want to waste time or energy on fishless waters. The units can also help one to find structure, drop-offs, and the like, and tell you the water's temperature and its depth.

There are several models on the market—Humminbird, Lowrance, Bottom Line, and others. They are from reasonably priced to way more then you need to spend. For the kayak I prefer a console model. Most makers offer portable versions of all their console models, or a twelve-volt rechargeable battery can power them. For salt water, which can be hard on gear and crafts, the console models with the transducer installed inside the craft (canoe or kayak), is the best way to go.

I install my monitor on the spot on the deck meant for a compass or other control within easy reach. I like the Scotty's swivel fish finder mount, which allows you to remove the finder when not in use.

Drilling a hole in your kayak will take some courage. I've already made the mistakes, although no serious damage was done. Remember to take your time—use an awl and a tape measure, and be careful in laying out and measuring.

A fish finder's monitor is where you view all pertinent information. The transducer, connected to the monitor by a wire, marks the fish and any underwater structure.

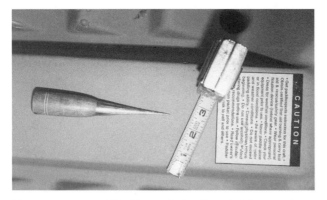

These are some of the items that will assist in ensuring that your drilling operations go smoothly.

A variety of drill bits, like those pictured here, will be necessary to complete your craft's customization.

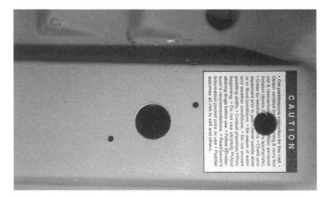

Well-placed, clean holes are a critical first step in the process of rigging your boat.

For my installation, I drilled two holes: a 7/8-inch one so I could run the connecting wires up from the hull, and a 1 3/8-inch hole for installing a Scotty flush mount. Using the flush mount for a guide to make sure of proper hole placement, I drilled two 3/16-inch holes as you see in the photo. I then used size 1/4-20 x1 (this is the most versatile size screw to use with Scotty rod mounts, from my experience) stainless steel screws, and nuts and bolts to bolt the mount down. I can now remove my monitor anytime I need to. I installed the transducer inside the hull of my kayak on the flattest area I could find. The simplest way to find that spot is to move the transducer around the inside of the hull until it rests flat without wobbling. Once the spot is located, trace around the transducer with a magic marker, and sand down the spot.

Cover the bottom of the transducer with silicone, place it down firmly on the marked spot, and tape it down with duct tape. Be generous—you do not want the transducer to shift. When this procedure is done let it dry for at least 24 hours before going on the water.

My fishing crate plays an important part in how I rig my kayak. It

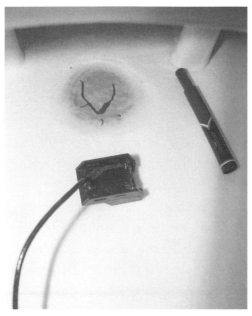

The transducer should be placed inside the kayak's hull on the flattest spot you can locate.

The transducer, taped in place while the sealant dries and sets.

The final setup. Now it's ready to locate some fish, or at least some places where they're likely to be.

My fishing crate, which began its life as a milk container but has found a higher calling.

was actually a milk crate at one time, but if you cannot acquire a milk crate, then a small square plastic laundry basket will do. Either of these, with its open-mesh construction, is less wind resistant, which is very important in a kayak. With a couple of pieces of 12-inch PVC pipe, four inches in diameter, secured with a hose clamp in each corner of your fishing crate, you have an extremely useful carrier for your net, cooler, tackle, anchor, and throw rope, on and off the kayak. To secure the fishing crate to a kayak without a tank well, simply run a couple of Bungee cords through the basket, and latch it down to the screw eyes. . . if you don't have them, install them. Another thing I do with a Bungee cord is wrap one around the outside of the crate (not too tight), to provide a temporary holder for nets, water bottles, paddle leash loops, tackle bags, fly boxes, and rods. (The fishing crate can be used just as easily on a pontoon boat or in a canoe.)

ANCHORING SETUPS AND TECHNIQUES

A student and friend purchased a fully rigged kayak from me, including my rolling pin anchor system. The following weekend, he, some of our fly-fishing club members, and I were going on a fishing trip down the Sacramento River. He and I would be the only kayakers; the rest of the group would be in pontoon boats. Having some concern over his lack of familiarity with the anchor system, I advised him to practice on friendly waters before doing any serious fishing trips with it. By the time the weekend arrived, early rains and family obligations compelled all of us, except my student and one other member, to cancel. The area where my student and the remaining club member launched on the river that day, the Sacramento's current was doing ten knots. If he had just paddled through the current, he probably would have made it. Instead, he did something foolish: he dropped his anchor. The purpose of this procedure is to slow down the kayak, so you have more casting time. This is a good technique, provided that you've had previous experience with your anchor and the river you're fishing. My student had neither. He hadn't gone a hundred yards in the strong current when the anchor lodged between some rocks or on other objects on the bottom of the river. As the kayak started to capsize from the pull of the rope, he dove in and swam to shore, and from there he watched as the kayak was pulled under the swift current. The anchor came loose once, but caught again and the kayak was pulled under once again. All the student came away from the Sacramento River with were the clothes he was wearing.

There are two things that the young man could have done to be better prepared for this situation. One would have been, as already mentioned, to have put in the appropriate practice time. The other would have been to have had the right equipment, such as a knife, handy. When your anchor gets you into trouble, a knife can free you from that trouble.

There's a happy ending to this story. Once off the river, the student called the local sheriff and reported the incident. The following day a couple of fishermen in a drift boat spotted the kayak, where it had washed up on shore. An abandoned kayak or any other craft usually means trouble, and fearing the worst, the fishermen called the same sheriff. The student got back everything except the top half of his new rod.

On my first day of fishing from a kayak, I learned how crucial having a good anchor setup was. Without it, the wind can blow you right over a school of fish you've just paddled within casting range of, or right on top of some lily pads where you wanted to cast your fly. Are you getting the idea? I found that a good anchor setup was crucial for the waters I would be fishing, and after quite a bit of trial and error, I designed the rolling pin anchor system.

For this setup, I have installed two latch downs, one on each end of my kayak (as close to the bow and stern, respectively, as possible) on the left side, and connected a pulley to each one. I then run a single length of no-stretch yacht rope, 3/16 inch in diameter, through the two pulleys. Each of the rope's two ends is tied with cinch knots to a triangle ring, such that the loop of rope (joined at the triangle ring) is reasonably taut. Next, I run the rope (to which the anchor will be attached) through the triangle ring. With this setup you can easily locate the anchor rope at the bow or at the stern. This has the advantage of actually allowing the wind to help you, not hinder you.

This is true because by selecting from which point of the craft the anchor is set, the wind (or current) will push the craft in whichever orientation

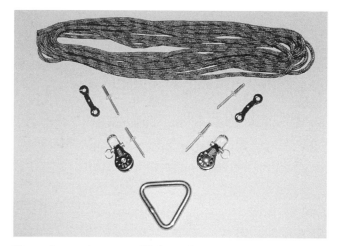

My anchor system uses 50 feet of no-stretch yacht rope, 3/16 inches in diameter.

is best for the particular fishing situation at hand, whereas in that same situation the opposite anchoring point would do the reverse and orient the craft opposite to that which best serves that scenario's needs. What has any of this got to do with rolling pins? To answer that question, we must first pose another: where does a 50-foot length of rope—as much as you should ever need for anchoring—go on a kayak? One fateful day while doing dishes, I was putting away silverware, when I noticed our rolling pin. Picking it up, I spun the roller while I held onto the handle in my hand, and the light bulb inside my head came on.

The metal mechanism inside the roller, enabling it to roll while I held the handle, would also permit me to wrap 50 feet of rope around the roller. I could place the rolling pin into a 12-inch piece of PVC pipe, four inches in

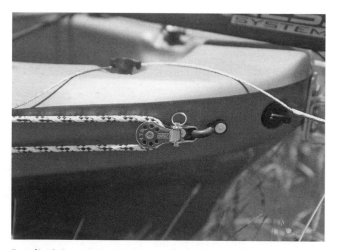

Detail of the anchor pulley. This system allows the boater to drop anchor from whichever spot along his craft's length he or she likes.

diameter, secured with a hose clamp in the corner of my fishing crate. When I lift the rolling pin by one handle only high enough so that the other handle is still inside the PVC holder, the weight of the sinking anchor will press the unit against the inside surface of the PVC pipe. This creates some friction, which slows the rope's unwinding, allowing the anchor to sink down smoothly in the water. If I jam the rope-wrapped rolling pin back completely into the PVC, it will behave like a brake, stopping the anchor's descent.

My rolling pin anchor setup uses a regular household rolling pin, which I stole out of my kitchen. My wife still hasn't missed it.

When I'm on a lake and I locate a good spot where I intend to anchor, I determine the wind's direction and position my kayak so that the wind is at my back. I then move my anchor to the stern—using the two-pulley system with triangular ring—and drop it, stay-

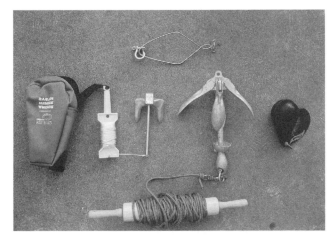

Anchor systems can come in a number of forms—weights, rolling-pin systems, clamps—depending on the craft, the types of places you fish, and your preferences.

ing enough distance from shore so that any trees or other land-based objects won't interfere with my casting.

I use a 5-pound folding anchor for lakes, flats, and mud bottoms. When I'm fishing rivers I use a 10-pound downrigger weight. For those times on big waters such as the ocean or large reservoirs when I just want to slow

my kayak down, I use a drift sock. Another tool that can function as a makeshift anchor is a clamp. With the clamp connected to the end of your anchor rope, you can keep your craft positioned on the edge of kelp beds, weed beds, lily pads, tules, or a tree or bush limb over a river or a pond. It should go without saying, of course, that one should pay attention to where the clamp is placed; one should watch out for nests, spider webs, and snakes.

Put a bit of a sidearm action in your cast while in the kayak, and you'll avoid hooking stuff in your kayak and yourself, and you'll also avoid putting a casting shadow directly over the fish.

Once you do start casting flies from a kayak, there will be new possibilities. Before we begin with casts you can do, however, there's a cast you shouldn't do anymore.

If you make a cast with your arm straight up while in your kayak, you are very prone to hook your fly on anything behind you. Therefore, the straight-up overhead cast that most of us do when we cast a fly line for the first time should be removed from your repertoire. Another disadvantage I've learned from my own experiences is that such a cast is an easy way to spook fish, either by lining them or by casting a shadow. A slight angle of your casting arm will increase hook-ups with fish, and decrease hook-ups on anything installed on your kayak behind you. . . and quite possibly yourself as well.

I've had a motorboat for the ocean and larger bodies of fresh water, or for covering long distances. For rivers and ponds I've used pontoon boats in various lengths, and I've used a canoe to pole up rivers as well as paddle down them. At one time I owned four different crafts. Now—I can simply paddle one properly rigged kayak to deliver my flies to the many different species of fish and the various types of water they swim in.

Your paddling skills are just as important as your casting skills. It will be a good stealth stroke that brings you within a forty-foot cast of midge-sipping trout, or stripers busting up a school of baitfish. It will be a good forward stroke that takes you across the lake to the headwaters where the big fish are feeding, and upriver to deliver your midge or streamer imitations to fool those wary trout. That same well-honed forward stroke will bring you back downriver and across the lake at the end of the day, feeling just as good as you did in the morning when you began.

The following is a useful example as to why you should take your paddling seriously and it should be second nature. One morning on my home water, Millerton Lake, I was fishing for spotted bass from my kayak, and I hooked a twelve-inch bass. After unhooking it, I put him back in the water to revive him and I placed my rod in its holder. He stayed where I placed him for a moment after I released him. I then noticed my fly was floating just a few inches behind the bass. Reaching for the fly, I got the scare of a lifetime—

about three feet of Mr. Linesides doing its imitation of a locomotive shot past, just inches from my kayak, inhaling the fish and my fly in one enormous gulp. By the time I'd recovered and my heart had starting beating again, the striped bass had taken an enormous amount of line, putting a definite bend in the rod. However, that rod was still in the holder, and I fumbled to get it out—not an easy feat with excessive striper poundage on the other end and headed in the opposite direction. Rod in hand, I strip set the hook—and the culprit and I were connected, although not for long. I heard the crack, and stared in horror at my two-piece rod—now a three-piece one—and a limp line empty of the striper that broke it.

What might have saved my dignity that day, and perhaps caught the fish as well, would have been the following sequence of actions. First, strip a bit of line off the reel, releasing some tension on the rod once I had it in my right hand. Next, tuck the paddle shaft under my right arm, holding it while bracing the blade with my left hand, and doing a backward stroke—thus turning the kayak around in the same direction as the big striper, giving me a fighting chance.

Once you hook a big fish while kayaking, these same paddling and fishing techniques will serve you well in fighting them. You will be able to back yourself out of situations such as leading a largemouth bass out of some weed beds or a lingcod from some kelp beds, or keeping a brown trout from swimming back into the rocks from which he emerged.

The following story will help to further illustrate some of these principles. One summer morning I was fishing on some private waters. Sitting in my kayak, my nine-weight rigged and ready, I was using a size 3/0 spinster (a fly tied on an Eagle Claw 413 Jig Hook, with a small spinner blade) I'd tied to look like a bluegill. I cast about thirty feet out and worked it back along the edges of the weed bed that ran along shore. A big splash several feet behind me startled me, and with a wide stroke with my paddle, the bow of my Tarpon 120 was pointing at the spreading ripples. One quick, short cast was all it took, and I was fighting a huge bass. As the battle went on, I heard several small splashes in a very small cove to the left of me. Another big bass had herded a bunch of bluegill into the small cove, and the hapless sunfish were splashing up out of the water to keep from becoming lunch. I could see the bass was big, as the top few inches of her was protruding above the surface, and her body was weaving back and forth as she fed on the 'gills.

A tug on my rod brought me back to reality, but the distraction was to prove costly. The bass pulled down, we engaged in a quick tug of war, and my line went limp. Quickly checking my leader, I saw my surgeon-knotted loop had broken right at the loop. My leader was ten-pound test fluorocarbon; I nipped off the broken loop, and tied on a new one. This time I tied on a twelve-pound tippet, and another spinster to that. I was going after the other bass in the little cove. I cast the spinster into the cove, and she took that fly and headed for another part of the lake, me and the kayak in tow.

After some heart-stopping hijinks, the line suddenly went limp. I started stripping in line, and felt it tug again on the other end, proof that she was still attached. Following my line by sight, I saw that it ended among some rocks just beneath the surface, about ten feet away. Paddling ever so slowly and stripping in line at the same time—yes, it can be done in a kayak—I closed the distance between the bass and myself. My leader, only a few inches from the side of my kayak, went straight down into what look like a pile of hydrilla. I held the rod up with one hand as high as I could while I removed the weeds with the other. The air was very heavy with tension. One last handful and there she was in view, for only a fraction of a second before she streaked off back the way we came. Once again I was being towed, only this time backwards. I put the paddle shaft under my right upper arm and did a forward sweep stroke, pulling hard on it with my left hand, causing the kayak to turn sharply and point it in the same direction the bass was going. As the kayak turned, it slowed down the fish.

The bass was just out of reach of my net. Trusting my knots, I started paddling backwards, rod in hand, shaft under my right upper arm, controlling the paddle blade with my left. When I had the bass far enough away from some threatening cover, I extended my rod back pulling her closer. I netted her on my second try, the biggest bass I've ever brought to net. . . at least, so far.

Trolling Your Fly. In the world of fly fishing, there are plenty of ways to be a "purist," and trolling a fly would probably be tops on the list of what these so-called purists would not consider to be fly fishing. It involves no casting or retrieving of line, nor does the user feel that beloved tug when a fish attacks the fly. It does, however, give the fly life as you paddle or row through the water. When any angler propels himself through the water, he is actually moving at the best speed to imitate fleeing prey like baitfish, crayfish, shrimp, and a host of others.

This technique blends kayaking and fishing together better than almost any other. Unless I see surface action immediately, I invariably begin a day's fishing with the kayak troll. Once I'm on the water, I cast several feet of line out and then lean the rod on my shoulder, right against my neck, so I can immediately feel any action in the rod. I then start paddling, trolling the line behind me and keeping an eye on the fish finder as I go.

As I paddle quietly over the water, the fly line is trailing at a length of anywhere from 20 to 60 feet. Whatever depth at which I want my fly to troll, I'll add twenty feet of line to that number—for example, if I want to troll at a depth of ten feet, I'll have thirty feet of line out. I wait for the fish finder to start registering fish, and when it does—without moving my rod—I gently paddle forward one stroke each hand, then one brace, and then repeat. With this technique I'm imitating a wounded baitfish, or a dragonfly nymph. For a fleeing baitfish, simply use a basic forward stroke. By using this and other similar strokes, I'm giving my fly life with the paddle, somewhat similar to stripping the line. The possibilities are endless. The International Game Fish Association might not accept this technique, but the fish certainly do.

Many times while paddling along at a decent speed, I've looked back after feeling my fly rod jerk to see a small spotted or stripe bass skimming across the surface, looking like someone on a personal watercraft for the first time. It's a different story when a big fish bites, however; I'm then reminded of the reasons I cast my flies from a kayak. A fish of just a few pounds has pulled my sixty-seven-pound kayak around in circles more than just a few times. When fishing from a kayak, the fight between fisherman and fish is definitely more equal. Bigger fish have caused some humorous results. . . not necessarily for me, but for anyone watching.

Much has been written about ways to avoid spooking schooling fish when boating. At the sound or vibration of a motor, any, say, stripers tearing up a school of shad will head downtown. In my experience, an electric motor will cause this even more quickly than a gas motor will. But in a kayak I can paddle right up to such a phenomenon and start casting. And it gets even better: I've learned when such a free-for-all is going on, if not disturbed by motorboats, this commotion will draw fish from all over the lake, causing the whole scene to erupt into a giant melee of fish eating fish.

When I cast right in the middle of one of these free-for-alls, I tend to catch the smaller fish in the school, which nail the fly before it can go deeper. When this happens, I'll then start working the edges of the school, about three feet away from all the commotion; success can be signaled by a jolt in my rod that moves my whole kayak.

FISHING TACTICS

Targeting Fish in Saltwater Tides

Using a kayak in a river or stream to prospect for fish and set up for making casts in current is much similar to what I discussed in the canoe chapter. A kayak might even be easier in that you can put the rod in the rod holder and quickly back-paddle, then put down the paddle, cast to targets A through C or D, and then back paddle again, cast again, and then maybe drift your way out the end of the run.

When it comes to fishing in salt water, you'll need to know the tides and watch the time. For instance, if the incoming tide is 4:30 a.m., outgoing is 2:00 p.m., that equals roughly seven hours to fish, and two and a half for paddling time. If you launch on a high tide, bear in mind that you might return on the low tide, and you could face a trek through thirty yards of impossible mud to get back to your launch point. Not good.

Check your watch before you start paddling, and when you reach your fishing destination, check it again. Then you'll know how much time you'll need to get back to the launch. If I don't stop to fish I can paddle a mile in a half hour. Don't exhaust yourself, because you've got to be able to get back.

That said, searching for and fighting fish can often draw you farther away from your launching point. Most often I search out foraging gamefish on a rising tide around sandbars, jetties, troughs and channels, drop-offs, and underwater structures.

Fish move in reaction to tides, and that influences greatly how you move with the tides. The main thing is to locate structure on moving tide, either incoming or outgoing. Gamefish hang out over or next to structure, waiting for baitfish to go by (the baitfish are either riding the current or chasing much smaller, drifting prey). But, similar to river fishing, you must be able to deal with and compensate for moving water. You might have to work a point several times, paddling back up-current to ride back down to make several casts. This affects greatly the kind of line you choose—sinking tip versus full-sinking line. A full-sinking line might get your fly down quicker, but pulling up all that heavier sinking line to make another quick cast to a target as you drift on the current might not be as easy as using a sink-tip. But, if you're in some deep water, getting the fly down on the first cast and letting it swim as you drift in the kayak and mend the line can allow you to cover a long section. So, know the depth, and have on hand a couple of different rods set up with various lines.

One of my favorite areas to fish in salt water is a bay. A bay can be a great area for your first time fishing from a kayak in salt water. You won't have to deal with intimidating surf. You can launch from any public launch in the bay, and paddle out to open water and back when the time is right.

My favorite bay to fish in California is Monterey Bay, and my favorite place to launch from is the Santa Cruz harbor.

I like to get to the water by dawn, when the marina's not crowded. My partner and I will lower our rudders and, watching our back casts, we start working the docks. There's a dock large enough to hold maybe 20 boats to my left. We're paddling against an incoming tide. I want to prospect the dock for some fish. I paddle past the dock and then turn, facing the dock, and I let myself drift to have time to study the place. As I drift, controlling my paddle with my left hand and my right elbow, I occasionally dip the paddle to slow the drift. In this situation, sometimes a simple roll cast will suffice to get a fly right up against the pilings.

When I do cast, I give the fly time to sink to the desired level, strip the line, and cast again. This fish prospecting technique works well for me along jetties, kelp beds, and shorelines, as long as the surf is agreeable.

Paddling out of the harbor on to open water, my fishing partner and I venture in water too deep to see any structure. This is a situation where I truly depend on a fish finder and once I mark fish, I'll troll a fly (see Chapter 5).

Fighting and Landing Larger Fish

Here's a quick story, with a moral attached: One morning I meant to take advantage of a half hour to fish in Monterey Bay before doing a kayak-fishing clinic. But a bunch of early arrivals in about ten kayaks quickly surrounded me. Leaving my fly in the water, I went ahead and started to answer my pupils' questions. I was in maybe 50 feet of water when my fish finder started beeping. As I checked the monitor I saw the depth gauge move from 49 to 10 feet, and just about the same time I felt my rod jerk in a way I had never felt before. Actually, that's not true—I hooked the back of a pickup on a back cast one time when I was practicing my casting in the front yard, and this was the exact same feeling.

Fortunately my bow was pointed in the right direction and I tie a decent Bimini knot when I build a fly line, because the creature on the end of my line yanked me out of my teaching circle, almost capsizing a couple of kayakers as it did so. Pushing the fighting butt of the rod into my gut, my PFD gave me the perfect cushioning and acted as a fighting belt. The mysterious fish was towing my kayak so fast the stern threw up a wake. I locked myself in with my thigh braces, which would help hold my course.

Then with both hands back on my rod I reeled in a few inches of line, no effect. Looking back over my shoulder the early arrivals were dots growing smaller in the distance. All I could do at this point was to be a human drag. My depth gauge had gone back to 50 feet, then to 80, and it was showing deeper with every glance.

The fish took me into my backing shortly after it pulled me out of the circle. Finally just when I thought it was starting to tire and slow down, I realized it was going down: straight down. Not at any time did I fight that fish from the side of my 'yak. I kept my rod parallel with the bow.

Pointing my rod tip in the direction of the fish, I reeled in what slack line there was, and then I straddled my 'yak and pulled back on the rod. The fish pulled back on the other end with enough force to pull me down against the cockpit of the kayak and make my drag sing like an insane bee. I was then officially scared.

My initial fantasies about being a modern Old Man in the Sea were gone. This was serious—too serious, I decided. But just when I was reaching for my knife to cut my line the sleigh-ride ended. I quickly reeled in my line. The 3/0 hook on which I'd tied something like a Deceiver was bare and completely straight. I found out later what I hooked was probably a shark or a big stingray, either one up to 100 pounds.

This is a true story, and a good example of what can happen in the salt. I'll remember that fish and the adventure it gave me for the rest of my life.

Now for the moral of the story:

I never could have landed that fish by myself, had I fought it to the surface and tried to take it—trying to might possibly have been fatal. So when you fish from a kayak in salt water, always go with a buddy. You could probably say that of any water, but in the salt, never go alone. And if you target fish that go over 50 pounds, maybe take a friend who has experience with such species, or hire a guide just to fish with you.

But if you're really serious, then the time will come when you've got a big fish by the side of the kayak, and you're going to find out just what sort of salty kayaker you are. My buddy Jeff "Rhino" Krieger handles big fish as well as anyone can. Jeff was one of the first kayak-fishing guides on the West Coast. Thresher sharks are his specialty, and his personal best is a 225-pound thresher. The biggest one he's hooked could have been 350 pounds.

Jeff has also taken yellowtail up to 25 pounds, white sea bass to 52 pounds, and halibut of 50 pounds. How does he do this?

Jeff makes great use of a drift chute or sea anchor. You tie this to the anchor line, and let it drift a few feet behind you. It will behave like a drag chute (as in drag car races) and slow you down considerably. When a big fish fights you, it must then battle the rod, drag, weight of the kayak, and the drag of the drift chute. Wear the fish down till it behaves like a dog that won't walk anymore. Once the fish tires you can reel it in alongside the kayak, where you can perform the PAR move: photograph and release. With really big fish, just leave them in the water and remove the hook with a long-handle hook-extractor tool. On fish that you can handle, use a BogaGrip to stabilize the fish for hook removal (this works fine for fish in the 20-pound range). Big nets can work, too, to keep a fish stable alongside the kayak. Now, Jeff has been known to lay a big fish over the beam of his kayak. That's a dicey move and I don't recommend it, because you can quickly roll yourself if you get into a brawl with a big fish on top of your kayak.

So, let the adventure begin. And that is what it will be, because you'll be paddling a craft in which the Inuit stalk seal, waterfowl, and caribou, and in which you can catch all manner of fish.

Safety 6

One Saturday I helped guide a group of first-time canoeists on their journey down the lower San Joaquin River. My job was to follow behind the group in my kayak, helping out the head guide and the clients that day. Our paddling caravan was a group of women ranging in age from 18 to 60, filling five canoes along with the head guide who shared the lead canoe with one of the ladies.

The guide, as all good guides should, instructed his group in paddling and safety techniques, telling them to wear their life jackets at all times, and not to stand up in the canoe. Later, as we began our trip down river, the head guide stood up in his canoe, which he did the entire trip, sitting

Safety first—always use your personal flotation device (PFD).

down only to paddle through the faster-moving runs and never once donning his life jacket.

When the trip was over and the ladies had departed, I asked him about his reasoning. After he described his familiarity with and knowledge of the river, as well as his swimming prowess, I suggested to him that none of his knowledge would do anybody any good if he were unconscious, a situation that could easily have happened to him while going down a river and standing in a canoe.

The ladies had had the good sense to wear their life jackets and sit down in the canoe, and fortunately nobody had to save Mr. Head Guide. What I hope is clear from this anecdote is that everyone should wear his or her life jacket at all times: boaters, canoeists, kayakers, fishermen, guides, and particularly head guides. Many people drown every year because their life jackets were just too uncomfortable to use, and kayakers and fishermen make up a lot of the statistics. You do not store the PFD somewhere handy on your kayak. . .You wear it.

Don't scrimp when it comes to buying your Personal Flotation Device (PFD). For around a hundred bucks you can buy one that's as comfortable as any fly fishing vest, with lots of arm room for paddling and casting. Pick one in a bright color (yellow and red are my choices) in order to maximize your visibility. My PFD took the place of my fly fishing vest—I use a retractor (that works like a tape measure) that clips on to my pocket and from which hangs my fishing license, a pair of line clippers, and safety whistle. I can reach any of them when I need them.

Two accessories that make a sit on top very effective as a paddling and fishing craft are a seat and a pair of thigh braces.

Next to your PFD, the seat is the most important accessory on your kayak. There are several makes on the market and they come in a variety of shapes, sizes, and colors. You can get them with holders for water bottles or fishing rods (although I haven't seen any for fly rods). Some models have a handy pocket on the back. My personal preference is a high-backed model with a pocket on the back big enough for one or two fly boxes. The seat should be adjustable, and take the time to ensure it's positioned for maximum comfort so you can paddle all day pain-lessly. In fact, it's prudent to adjust your seat the minute you sit down in it to begin a day of paddling and casting. I like my seat adjusted almost straight up, with just a bit of a back-wards lean to it. Keeping the posture that's best for you can make a huge difference, as one incident I recall shows.

On that occasion, part way through the day I started feeling a small pain in my lower back, due to the fact my seat wasn't adjusted properly. It was just a little pain, so foolishly I didn't worry about it. After a day of decent fish-ing, my companions and I paddled back to the spot from which we'd launched. I was still feel-ing that little pain as I paddled into shallow water. Throwing my legs over the side of my kayak, and putting my feet on solid ground, I slowly tried to straighten up and stand from the sitting position I was in, but I was unable to. My body was locked in a sitting position. I

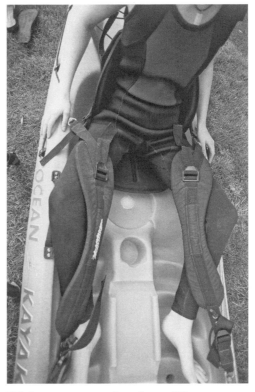

Thigh straps can make a huge difference in efficiency and comfort when using a sit-on-top kayak.

had to exert extreme efforts to gain the shore, not an easy thing to do when frozen in a sitting position. After finally recovering from that distress, I checked my seat out and saw the reason. The adjustments on my seat caused me to lean forward a bit, and paddling in that position for several hours was what caused my lower back to freeze. When you feel any pain while paddling, stop and figure out what it is.

Thigh braces are very important accessories. Because of them, my pad-dling is just as effective in a sit-on-top as it is when I paddle one with a cock-pit. It often amazes me how many paddlers have no idea what thigh braces are. Most SOTs come from the factory rigged for thigh braces, and many peo-ple mistake the screw eyes intended for the braces, for the ones intended for the seat. Thigh braces do for a paddler in an SOT what a cockpit does for a sea kayaker. In the cockpit of a sea kayak, a paddler can brace his knees against the deck (there's usually foam installed under the deck for that purpose) and add more power and effectiveness to his paddle stroke. With thigh braces in an SOT, you will have the same advantage.

Don't forget your safety whistle. On another guided canoe trip, in which I again provided rear support but this time on Millerton Lake, it was windy on the water that day. Everyone was paddling hard to stay on course. I looked for the head guide, only to notice him running along the bank and yelling instructions at a mother and son, who were hanging on for dear life while their canoe was being blown back the way we had come. The paddlers in another canoe were going to try to help, while the others didn't know where they were going and they were getting blown around as well. The best thing to do in that situation or any one like it is simply to get off the water.

I yelled "off the water!" a couple of times, but got no response. I took my rescue whistle out of my pocket and blew on it. Everyone looked in my direction. I pointed my paddle toward the shore, started paddling that way, and the others followed me in. The mother and son were rescued by a couple of kayakers that were tagging along for the tour.

If you're in trouble and you can't yell loud enough, you can probably whistle loud enough. Safety whistles can be had for around five bucks, and there are no excuses to be without one.

What about a knife? A good choice is one with a serrated and normal blade combination, with a plastic sheath including belt loop attachment so that it can be worn on your PFD or somewhere else handy, for cutting tangled fishing line, anchor ropes, and a host of other reasons. A knife is simply a good tool to have.

WADERS, ANORAKS, WADING JACKETS, AND WET SUITS

Waders are certainly necessary for those of you who choose to sit in the water in your tube or on top of it in your kick boats and cast your flies. However, if you decide to move up above the water level in a canoe or kayak, those trusty waders will serve you just as well. A pair of good quality waders, breathable or neoprene, can do the job. (The breathable stocking-foot type, not the boot-foot type, is the only kind I recommend.) One of the many pluses about them is you can layer clothing under them and still be comfortable, and then remove layers as the weather warms. The waders I wear are durable, with built-in side straps for a wader belt, and do wear one—it'll keep the water out if you wind up in the water.

Before we move on to other apparel, I'd like to dispel an old myth. If you fall in the water with waders on, you don't sink to the bottom. So that I would not have any doubts if an immersion situation ever happens (such as my canoe or kayak capsizes), I gave myself a test. Attired in my Polartec long johns, my fleece sweat suit, high-tec waders, Anorak jacket over that, and my PFD topping it all off (which, by the way, when worn over waders keeps out water better than any belt), I jumped into a swimming pool. I didn't sink like a rock at all; in fact, I floated like the Pillsbury doughboy. I swam and floated around for about a half hour, more than enough to do a self-rescue. . . provided you know how, and you've practiced doing one in the first place.

For cold-weather kayak fishing, such as for fast-moving rivers, the ocean, and winter fishing in general, my outfit is the same one I wore when I jumped in the pool.

What about warm weather? Summer is when I exchange my waders for quick-drying clothing made of nylon until the waters cool again. Nylon dries quickly; you can go from soaked to dry within a half hour, half of my wardrobe is made of it and it has a high UPF (Ultraviolet Protection Factor) rating for sun protection.

Anoraks, Wading and Paddling Jackets. Over my waders or wetsuit, I wear my Breeze paddling jacket made by Kokatat—for colder weather and waters my Anorak. They both wear well in rainy weather also. I prefer a paddling jacket or an Anorak, because they are made so you can wear a PFD over them comfortably. Anoraks and paddling jackets are designed with a lot of freedom in the arm and shoulder area, so that paddlers can paddle comfortably, a design that will benefit any kayak fisherman's casting.

Using the right equipment, including apparel, for the right purpose is beneficial for any pastime. A good paddling jacket will enable you to concentrate on the paddling and fishing rather than the elements.

It's also possible to go the wetsuit route in this endeavor. The best style of wetsuit for paddling fisher's are Farmer Johns, which are sleeveless, leaving room for paddling and casting. You can buy a good-quality wetsuit for around a hundred dollars. While my waders can do the job, I don't like the idea of exposing them to salt water. A well-fitted wetsuit is like a second skin, and is my preference for those monthly trips to the Pacific Ocean.

Having the means of staying comfortable while kayaking can substantially extend your season of enjoyment. For me, fall doesn't mean the beginning of winter; it means unlimited fishing possibilities and lakes and rivers empty of personal watercraft and speedboats. On a cold fall morning, on Millerton Lake—California's tenth largest reservoir—my kayak has been the only craft on the water. I've seen a mountain lion chase deer along the shore not more then a hundred feet from my kayak. I've watched an eagle pluck a bass from the water. Mornings like that are one of the sparks that continually feed my flame of inspiration that kayak fishing continues to give me.

To top it all off, let's talk about hats. Out on the water in warm or even hot weather (in the center of California where I live that can be pretty hot), without a hat on your head a sunburn will occur very quickly. Wear a hat and keep the sun off your head, and if you're casting flies from a kayak, it provides an additional modicum of protection for keeping the fish hooks out of your scalp.

I've never been a big fan of baseball-style caps, as they do not protect your ears from the sun or hooks. My preference is brimmed hats—not hard-brimmed hats as they can behave like a sail when the winds comes, but soft-brimmed ones instead.

When the weather gets really cold, your-ears-and-nose-hurt type of cold, the hooded Anorak really comes into its own. Two other items a whole lot cheaper then anything else in a paddling fishermen's wardrobe can be a stocking cap or a bandana. On those cold, cloudy, windy, and sunless days, a wool stocking cap will take care of you nicely. Some people prefer fleece as a substitute. Another alternative, especially for those days the wind seems incessant, is a bandana, which protects the head from the sun and has no brims to catch those breezes.

Another item I discovered since I took up the kayak is wet boots. Wet boots are like wading boots, only better. They are more comfortable, nowhere as bulky, provide much better traction (slippery felt soles do not belong in canoes or kayaks), and cost less. They come in plenty of styles, from a shoe to a knee-high

For the ultimate in elemental protection, consider a wetsuit.

A bandana is a good choice for headgear that will provide some protection from the sun but be less subject to sudden gusts of wind.

Wet boots: a slimmer, more comfortable, and higher-traction choice than wading boots.

boot. I like the boot style, about nine inches high with a side zipper, which fit quite comfortably over my stocking-foot waders.

Another important consideration is sunscreen. Sitting in a kayak, particularly a sit-on-top on the water on a warm day, a fair-skinned person without proper protection, sunscreen, or clothing can burn to a nice red tone within a couple of hours. My personal preference is BullFrog, which is also available in a spray bottle. (A word to the wise: handle sunscreen around your fly gear carefully, as it can melt some fly lines.)

No fisherman should be without polarized sunglasses. Otherwise, the water surface will be just a glare, and your eyes will be unprotected from fishing lures flying through the air. On the water, make sure your glasses are on floating retainers, and if you're an official "four eyes" like myself, carry spares in your ditty bag.

Ditty bag: the paddler's purse. Actually a small dry bag, small enough to fit inside your fishing crate or hatch. It should include signaling devices, mirror, whistle, horn, flares, waterproof matches, and an extra set of clothing.

The throw rope has helped more than one paddling fisherman out of tight spots, and is worth considering as a part of your craft's complement of equipment Consider the following scenario. Two paddling fishermen are on a river; one is experienced and one is not. Paddler number one has paddled through some areas with a mixture of obstacles, rocks, and eddies; he has gotten a boost to his confidence, and a shot of adrenaline. Paddler number two is apprehensive and feeling intimidated. After watching paddler one go through a short run of rapids, working through the eddies, dodging the boulders, and in general making it look easy, paddler two is ready to try. Paddler one has paddled through the run, and is out of the water, standing on shore, ready with a throw rope in case paddler two gets into trouble. If so he can throw the rope and pull paddler two out of it.

This can also function as a tow rope. For a number of reasons—your paddling partner loses his paddle, he's unable to keep up, he gets separated from his kayak (which can be serious business), he gets injured (dislocated shoulder, hit in the face or head)—you should have a tow rope.

For rivers and flat water, the throw rope will be more than adequate. On the ocean you will want to downsize to a smaller rope, which can be stored more easily than a throw rope. The recommended length for a tow rope is fifty feet. Tie loop knots on each end to which you can attach carabiners, and you'll have a good setup.

Other items that can make a significant difference are a compass, VHF or two-way radios, Global Positioning System (GPS) unit, and ditty bag for storage. On familiar waters these items might not seem important. If, for instance, you launch from your favorite harbor or marina and are headed for those well-known kelp beds, you won't be that far from shore. The situation may seem harmless enough, but if a fog rolls in unexpectedly and now you can't see the shore, then things are suddenly very different.

On a VHF or two-way radio, the Coast Guard and most vessel traffic authorities monitor channel 16 for maydays and emergency distress calls, and there are channels specifically for weather and tides. On other channels you can communicate with fishing buddies, listen to fishing reports, or let a yacht know it's about to run over you. You can now buy a two-way VHF radio for around a hundred bucks. Considering that a VHF radio could save your life, and has saved many others, there is no excuse not to have one. There are a number of waterproof bags for radios on the market. Put your radio or your cell phone in one and keep it handy. Other items that should also be in your ditty or rescue bag are signaling devices, mirror, whistle, horn, flare, waterproof matches, and an extra set of clothing.

Whatever craft you choose, always be prepared. When a float tube or pontoon happens to spring a leak, or when your canoe or kayak decides to capsize, that extra set of clothing and that radio or the flares that you had in the ditty bag could save your life.

Accessories 7

od Holders, Leashes: Rod holders are simply part of a well-organized fishing craft. Besides being a place to put your rod when you're paddling, they are the only safe way to carry more than one rod and will save rods in many cases if you capsize your craft. I have found that Scotty Rod Holders are the best ones for any kayak on the water.

They are adjustable, from a ninety to a forty-five degree angle. (One of the benefits of the lower angle is that your spare rods will be out of the way of your back cast.)

Leashes. When I fish from a sit-on-top kayak, both my fly rods have leashes on them, as well as my paddle. The fly rod with which I am fishing is leashed to a screw eye on the right side of my kayak, while the paddle is leashed to one on the left. With the exception of my paddle leash, all of them are commercially made coiled ones. With some knot knowledge, a couple feet of rope, and two leash hooks, you can make leashes for whatever your needs may be (I have a leash on anything that can sink). It doesn't take long to get used to casting with a leash on your rod; however, it does take a while to get over the pain of losing a rod because you did not have a leash on it.

The rod holder should be an essential component of your craft's rigging complement no matter which style of boat you choose. Pictures here are versions for the float tube (left), pontoon boat (right), canoe (middle), and kayak (bottom).

There are paddlers that wouldn't think of using a leash in a kayak, particularly in the sea. If you capsize, you don't want anything you'd tangle up in. Considerations such as these suggest keeping the number of leashes used to a minimum, in contrast to earlier concepts. It is up to each user to determine the balance that works best for him- or herself.

I've found that a number of experienced paddlers leash their paddles to their wrist when they're on the water, and they also

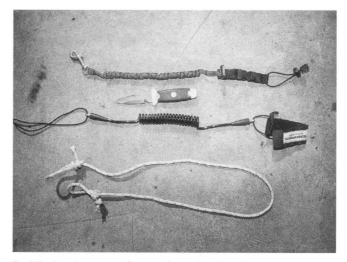

Paddle leashes come in a variety of styles, but they all keep you from being stuck up a creek without a paddle.

carry a spare paddle. When they practice capsizing their sea kayaks, they tuck the paddle under their arm. The first time I practiced capsizing with my paddle leashed to my kayak, the paddle shaft hit me in the head. I now leash it to my wrist.

My paddle leash is 30 inches long, using 3/8-inch diameter, non-stretch yacht rope, with a non-slip loop tied on one end—big enough so that my hand can slip in and out effortlessly. A Duncan loop (a slip loop similar to a hangman's noose) is on the end I leash to my paddle. When I'm paddling a sit-on-top, I leash my paddle to my wrist. Those times when I stand in a kayak to cast or pole, I stick the hand loop of the paddle leash in that Bungee cord that's around my fishing crate where it can be pulled free in an emergency. Whatever craft I paddle, I always have a spare paddle.

Paddle Clips. Installed properly, paddle clips can be quite useful for holding paddles or fishing rods. Properly placed paddle clips can be the best place for a rod, when you're going in and out of the surf. Installed poorly, you will hit the paddle clip with your paddle or wrap your fly line around it. I have both a landing net and a BogaGrip. As far as a landing net goes, on the

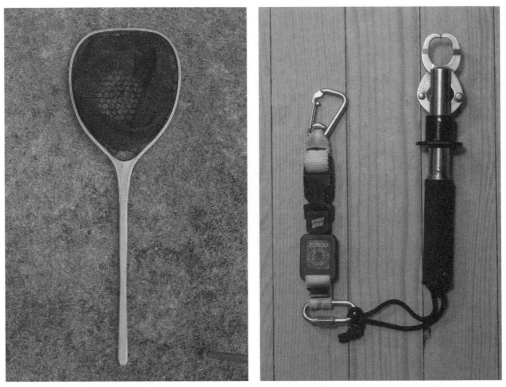

Whichever craft you choose, when the moment comes for you to secure your fish, I highly recommend a long-handled net.

The BogaGrip is a very handy tool, and I highly recommend its use.

Pacific Coast all crafts including kayaks have to have them. I've always preferred long-handled nets, with about two feet of handle. I've used this style of net for over thirty years; they've come in handy in numerous situations. With a long-handled net you do not have to lean out to net your fish, something best avoided in a kayak.

Using a net properly is not instinctive for most people. I begin with the net in my non-rod hand, and hold the rod up horizontally but as high up as I can, as I plunge the net into the water, right against the side of my kayak, so that my hand goes right to the water surface. I then begin to tilt my rod upward, making the fish come toward me. As the fish comes in, I tilt the net upwards as well to capture the fish. With this technique I end fights quickly, net a lot more fish, and release them in much better condition than they would have been after a long and strenuous fight.

Correct netting technique doesn't come immediately to many people, but if you follow the guidelines here it should come to you easily enough.

BogaGrip. When the fish is too big for the net, I have always lipped them when practical, although not without fear. A huge fish thrashing and splashing around with a hook in its lip is intimidating. The folks at BogaGrip have created a remarkable tool, with which a fisherman can reach out and lip his or her fish without fear of being hooked along with the catch. The unit is also a scale, which can be certified by the IGFA (International Game Fish Association).

Dry bags can provide good protection. They come in all shapes and sizes. You can get them in cylinder and triangle shapes, and may be small enough for your cell phone or big enough for a sleeping bag and a tent.

For real protection, I use Pelican Cases; I haven't carried my photography gear in anything else. Some of their products are waterproof in depths over a hundred feet.

Transporting a kayak is more manageable than many of the other small craft out there, but there are nevertheless some approaches that simplify it even more. One 'yak accessory that makes life easier is a dolly, a folding frame with wheels, that you can slip right over the bow, enabling you to pull your vessel like a wagon. There will be times when the distance to the water is too far to carry the kayak, even with help. In those cases, I think you'll agree that kayak dollies are worth their weight in gold.

Effective gear storage is something that has the potential to make or break your day. Give it some proper thought and preparation and you'll thank yourself later.

Pelican cases come in all sizes.

A dolly is a convenient means of transporting your craft overland some distance, and many models can fold right up for easy storage.

A couple of storage hooks installed a few feet apart in the ceiling or the wall of your garage, straps and you'll have a home for your 'yak.

When using your car or truck to transport your kayak, there are several choices, from a couple of pieces of soft foam and some rope, to racks, or you can purchase a kayak trailer (a real luxury).

Because they can be deflated, transporting float tubes or pontoon boats isn't much of a problem. Moving your canoe or kayak from home to water can be, but it is easily solved by a roof rack on top of your car or—even better—a trailer behind it. Years ago, when I was still using a ten-foot pontoon boat, I got tired of setting it up on the water and wasting fishing time, so I purchased a Thule cargo rack and installed it on top of my truck's camper shell. After that I was able to load my fully assembled pontoon boat on my shell, saving about an hour's worth of fishing.

I'm still using that same rack today, years later, for my canoe and kayaks. The best and safest way to load your canoe or kayak on top of your vehicle by yourself is put one end on a piece of scrap carpet or, even better, foam. Next, lift up the other end (using your knees, not your back) to the rack. Now pick up the end resting on the foam and slide it up on to the rack.

I prefer to load my canoe or kayak upside down on the rack; it's safer and easier to tie down securely.

If your budget allows and you have the room, a trailer is the easiest way to go, and your back will thank you. Any of the crafts discussed in this book can be carried, or all at the same time plus a few others.

We're talking about trailers made for carrying fishing and paddling crafts like the ones in this book. Over the years, I have found that loading a couple of 'yaks on top of my camper shell rack wasn't too bad. But loading a third kayak on top of those two, and then taking them down at the end of a day of guiding, was the hardest work I did all day. The first time I did a clinic and took all six of my kayaks was the last straw. It took about 45 minutes to load them all side by side, and that's a waste of fishing time—if you have a bad lower back, it's that much worse. I thought about buying a trailer and customizing it for my needs but even a basic trailer was over $1,000.

If you go the trailer route, search for the model that serves your needs best. The Slick Rydr **KMUT-0004** pictured here enables me to transport multiple craft at the same time.

What I wanted was a trailer capable of carrying about ten kayaks, onto which one person could load kayaks by himself. One thing I learned while doing my research was that they have the right shock absorbers—kayaks can bounce up and down quite a lot. My search led me to the company Slick Rydr, and I've been towing the KMUT-004 model for a few years now.

For the first time since I started conducting kayak fishing seminars, I did not need help loading up my kayaks. My trailer is a perfect display for the kayaks when I do a seminar or sports show, and when I need to work on a kayak the KMUT-0004 is just the right height. And the kayaks can be stored properly, ready to go any time you are. I must admit I did have a fear of towing a trailer.

If you obtain a trailer and are unfamiliar with maneuvering one, it is prudent to spend some time practicing. After several hours of practice backing up (and amusing the neighbors), I'm fine now at the boat launch as long as I don't panic.

Index

TELL THE WORLD THIS BOOK WAS

GOOD	BAD	SO-SO

About the Author

Throughout his life Rickey Noel Mitchell has paddled and cast from all forms of paddle crafts, from handmade rafts to pirogues. He is a freelance writer, photographer, and guide based in Fresno, California, where he has worked for the last several years combining his two passions—fly fishing and paddling. Mitchell gives talks and seminars at hunting and fishing shows on fly

fishing from personal fishing crafts and hosts his own Web site: www.paddleandflies.com. You can find his articles, critiques, and photos in various magazines, including *California Fly Fisher*, *Paddler*, and *Kayak Fisherman*.